FIRST-CENTURY JUDAISM
IN CRISIS

FIRST-CENTURY JUDAISM IN CRISIS

Yoḥanan ben Zakkai and the Renaissance
of Torah

JACOB NEUSNER

ABINGDON PRESS

Nashville   New York

FIRST-CENTURY JUDAISM IN CRISIS

Library of Congress Cataloging in Publication Data
NEUSNER, JACOB, 1932-
    First century Judaism in crisis.
    "Abridgement and condensation of A life of Rabban Yohanan ben Zakkai, ca. 1-80 C. E. (Leiden: E. J. Brill, 1962)
    Includes bibliographical references.
    1. Johanan ben Zakkai, d. ca. 80. 2. Judaism—History —Talmudic period, 10-425. I. Title
BM755.J7N42   296.6'1 [B]   74-14799

ISBN 0-687-13120-0

MANUFACTURED BY THE PARTHENON PRESS AT
NASHVILLE, TENNESSEE, UNITED STATES OF AMERICA

In memory of
ABRAHAM JOSHUA HESCHEL

CONTENTS

PREFACE

Coming to maturity at one of the great turning points in the history of Judaism, Rabban Yohanan ben Zakkai set the course followed by subsequent generations for many centuries. While the faith of Israel undoubtedly has been enriched by many other figures from biblical times to our own day, none apart from Moses and Jeremiah held such extraordinary responsibility. Second to these two alone, unendowed with prophetic gifts and therefore without the assurance afforded to the prophet by the Divine word, Yohanan guided both the faith and the people of Israel beyond the disaster of the destruction of the second temple and then laid foundations which have endured to this very day.

We know only a few of the barest facts about him. We do not know what he looked like or how he lived from day to day. We do not even know what he thought about many of the great issues of his day. Had he lived in some less interesting time, he would have been unknown in life, forgotten afterward. His kind of sober, irenic wisdom in politics, combined with intense religious concern, does not usually produce a broad reputation or vivid memories. We know for certain only this, that when everyone else had given up hope, Yohanan found reason to persevere. A man who overcomes despair in a time of disaster and keeps his eye upon the important matters in a day of confusion—does it count that we know a little of what he said and not at all what he looked like?

In the first century men generally regarded religion as an irreducible historical reality. For the most part they did not try to explain it as a consequence of economic, social, or psychological causes. For Jews, Scripture embodied the record of man's genuine religious experience. Therefore they looked into its ancient literature to find paradigmatic instruction on the nature of religion. They did so through the medium of disciplined exegesis, called *midrash* (from *darash,* "to search"). "The word of God is like fire," the Jewish sages taught, "and like the hammer that breaks the rock into pieces." No word of Scripture could therefore fail to yield a particular nuance of light, and, properly understood, none was irrelevant to events at hand. Some men were prepared to give their lives for scriptural imperatives. If today men die for nation or class, one legitimately turns to study the sources of nationalism or class loyalty. In the first century men died for faith. What was the content and direction of that faith? How did Jews mediate between the unchanging word of scriptural religion and the inconstant world in which they lived? We turn to the lives of those who best exemplified the religion of their time, for from the perspective of a later day, a few men appear to have embodied major elements of scriptural faith and experience, providing a living *midrash* of Scripture by reenacting a part of the biblical drama in their own age and idiom. Yoḥanan was one such man. His direct religious experience drew, in part, on the scriptural symbols provided by Ezekiel's vision of the chariot. His social and political thought finds significant parallel in the teachings of Jeremiah at the fall of the first temple in 586 B.C. His response to the destruction of the second temple in A.D. 70 recalls the capacity to seize upon disaster to transform religious understanding exhibited by Hosea before the fall of Samaria and by Second Isaiah in the Judean Exile in Babylon. His constructive activity at Yavneh bears comparison to that of Ezra in Jerusalem. Yoḥanan thus provides an interesting example of the structure of a scripturally-centered religious experience. Moreover, he was one of the leaders of the Pharisaic community in Jerusalem before the destruction of the Temple, and afterward he undertook the work of reconstruction.

This book does not offer a full-length portrait of Yoḥanan ben Zakkai. Such a portrait is not possible, for, as I said, the sources do not provide us with adequate information. Moreover, we have not yet found a convincing way of isolating earlier from later traditions about him except in a few instances, and we have no way of determining their historical accuracy. I have discussed the issue more fully in "In Quest of the Historical Rabban Yoḥanan ben Zakkai," *HTR*, 59 (1966) :391-413, and in *Development of a Legend: Studies on the Traditions Concerning Yoḥanan ben Zakkai* (Leiden: E. J. Brill, 1970). As Professor Judah Goldin writes in Charles J. Adams, ed., *A Reader's Guide to the Great Religions* (New York: 1965) :

> Not only do the primary sources disappoint us deeply in the amount of reliable *historical* detail they provide, but even as regards the opinions and teachings of the Sages, one is left to guess as what is early and what is late. In short, there is practically no way to get at *development* [p. 223].

Goldin rightly stresses that such a work as this is filled with speculation. It is useful mainly as a collection of sources about a specific sage.

I have tried to organize the extant data quoted or cited in the pages that follow according to historical and sociological principles. I have grouped the stories dealing with various periods of Yoḥanan's life in the temporal sequence I believe obviously appropriate, even though these stories certainly did not originate in such an orderly, historical way. Chapters two, three, six, seven and eight provide a chronological narrative of Yoḥanan's education, early career in Galilee, years in Jerusalem, activities during the war of 66-73, and later leadership at Yavneh. I have analyzed Yoḥanan's religious ideas according to Max Weber's insights concerning the tension between charisma and routine within religious life.

As I see it, Yoḥanan encountered a highly spontaneous kind of Judaism in his Galilee years and a thoroughly routinized faith in Jerusalem afterward. The Pharisaic religion of "Torah," represented by Yoḥanan ben Zakkai, constitutes a synthesis between the two polar principles. Routine is imposed by the requirement to regularly study a given text. Spontaneity and charisma emerge in two ways: first, in the very content of the biblical text, which embodies the highly charismatic experiences of earlier ages; second, in the unexpected and unpredictable response of the sage to the text. This synthesis is described in chapter three. Its social consequences are treated in chapter four, and the hermeneutical and mystical aspects in chapter five. The last four chapters provide a view of how the religion of "Torah" guided Yoḥanan's thought and action in response to great historical events, theological issues, and social problems.

By forming the historical material into such a paradigmatic structure for religious-sociological investigation, I have probably forced it to conform to a much too neat ideal type. But this has provided the possibility of reaching more useful insights into the history of first-century Judaism than are to be gained from a mere rehearsal of texts. The reader, however, is warned that it is I who see Yoḥanan's Galilee and Jerusalem years as encounters with antithetical principles in religious life, and his subsequent career in teaching and leadership as a synthesis of them. My *interpretation* of the literary data has imposed this structure. For me, and I hope for the reader, it brings a measure of order out of chaos. That interpretation offers an opportunity to use a fruitful sociological theory in studying otherwise unrelated stories and sayings. But we cannot confuse interpretation of texts not yet subjected to careful form-critical studies with sound, positive history. An historical evaluation of what Yoḥanan "really" said and did must await the results of other kinds of inquiry than are represented in this book.

Perhaps a personal word may not be out of order. Many years ago, when I began my studies of Yoḥanan ben Zakkai, I was drawn to him out of the deepening gloom of the Cold War. Day by day one looked to the skies, fearful of sighting that single plane bearing a single bomb to end the life of the city. What struck me then was the challenge of "the next day," the 10th of Av in Yavneh, or who knew what date the stars then would designate. He who had passed through that awful time would bear witness that life could go on, in new forms to be sure, and that men confidently might look beyond disaster. Now, again men stand at a crossroads, but the ways come from other directions and meet in a new locale. The issue of the day is different. We witness the ripping apart of the social fabric. In response we seek a nonviolent (so strangely negative a formula) way in violent times. The society of men and nations imposes upon our consciousness the single, compelling issue of how to abide with one another in conflict, yet not through mutual annihilation. Since nations and social groups have the power to destroy one another, we need to find new ways of expressing natural conflicts and resolving them in perfect peace. Renunciation of power and affirmation of the force of powerlessness—these are the challenges of the new apocalypse. The Yoḥanan of the year 70 therefore matters less today than the man of 'Arav and Jerusalem. Looking backward, we find an earlier climax in his life than the one I had once supposed. It does not come at the end of his life, or with the end of time as men had known it. It comes in the skeptical, detached, sorrowful, yet engaged and effective years before Yavneh. I once assigned him greatness with glory, but now understand the glory came before the greatness, before Yavneh. In the end came the honor and the fame, but now I see the fame mattered very little, to him perhaps not at all. Dignity without reward—this is the Yoḥanan for the present hour. What shall we perceive a decade hence? The sources stand, provoking in us a few enigmatic thoughts, providing us with far less than we need to know. The man remains well beyond our grasp, yet, I think, always near the center of our situation. The reason is that the centuries—his and ours—are not dissimilar.

This book is an abridgement and condensation of *A Life of Yoḥanan ben Zakkai, Ca. 1-80 C.E.* (Second edition, completely revised, Leiden: E. J. Brill, 1970; first edition: 1962). The beginning of form-critical study is in *Development of a Legend: Studies on the Traditions Concerning Yoḥanan ben Zakkai* (Leiden: E. J. Brill, 1970). Further methodological experiments along these lines are in my *Rabbinic Traditions about the Pharisees before 70* (Leiden: E. J. Brill, 1971, I-III),

Eliezer ben Hyrcanus: The Tradition and the Man (Leiden: E. J. Brill, 1973, I-II) and *A History of the Mishnaic Law of Purities* (Leiden: E. J. Brill, 1975. I-III: *Kelim.* IV-V: *Ohalot.* VI-VIII: *Negaim*). I am grateful to Mr. F. C. Wieder, Jr., Director of E. J. Brill, for permitting me to publish an abbreviation of the larger work on Yoḥanan ben Zakkai. Notes, references, bibliography, and technical discussions will be found in *A Life of Yoḥanan ben Zakkai,* available at E. J. Brill, Leiden, Holland. Here I have omitted all but the narrative and reference to sources.

J.N.

PROLOGUE
"I was asking the gods for you"

The story is told of a wonder-working philosopher, Apollonius of Tyana, who refused to set foot in Palestine during the Roman siege of Jerusalem. His reason was that the "land had been polluted by its inhabitants, both through what they had done and through what they had suffered." Throughout the empire, the unruly Palestinian Jews had become a byword, even before their Temple was destroyed and many of them were enslaved. Vespasian, the conqueror of Jerusalem, was renowned as a man of probity and wisdom, who followed Apollonius' advice "to destroy not the great but the hostile, to be ruled by laws, to serve the divinity, to attend to matters of government as a king but to his body as a private citizen, to teach imperial slaves and free servants appropriate humility, to send out as governors men who at least knew the languages of the territories they were to govern."

When Vespasian met Apollonius in Egypt, he implored him, "Make me emperor."

The latter replied, "I have already done so, for when I prayed for an emperor righteous and noble and temperate and gray-haired and the father of legitimate sons, I was asking the gods for you."

Vespasian answered that he hoped he might rule wise men and be ruled by them. He promised the assembled Egyptians, "You may draw on me as on the Nile."

Such was the man whom Jews have cursed for centuries as the destroyer of Jerusalem, whose son Titus burned the Temple. The wise philosopher praised as righteous, noble, and temperate, a man who, doing his duty, destroyed the Jewish revolutionary armies, and whose troops bravely exterminated the brave defenders of Masada. The great empire, which had brought prosperity to the far corners of the Mediterranean, saw the Jews as a contentious race. Rome regarded their unhappy fate as a justly merited punishment. So deep was the Jews' disaster that their land was seen to be polluted by their blood as much as by their deeds. The day of their disaster was celebrated as a grand triumph in the imperial city. So ambiguous was the hour that forty generations debated its meaning. How did it come to pass that men thus greatly misunderstood one another? How shall we explain the reverence of some for a man hated and cursed by others?

A Roman centurion landing at Caesarea in the middle of the first century must have wondered at the enmity he saw and felt among the Jews he had come to police. Doing his duty, he met men who thought that duty evil. Come to bring peace, he encountered people who wanted only to create disorder. Temperate and sober, as befitted a centurion of the universal empire, he saw a nation whose excitability bordered on the irrational. To him and his cohorts the Jews seemed never to be satisfied, no matter how carefully the government respected their rights and sensibilities. Jews hardly appreciated that Rome stood not as despotic ruler of internal matters, but as protector of world peace and guarantor of religious freedom. Rome was eager only to find the right men to rule each country in the right way. She had tried every possible means of keeping Palestine's Jews happy. At first she had ruled through the traditional high priests, then had supported a shrewd and particularly able man, Herod, when he came to power as ally of Rome and protector of Jewry. Herod had done everything within his power to win approval, but all to no avail. When he died, some rejoiced. Few mourned. Seeing the incompetence of his sons, the Romans had sent their own agents, procurators, who also tried to please the people, but with even less success. "What do these Jews want," the centurion must have wondered, "and what keeps them in ceaseless turmoil?"

A Caesarean Jew, living in a mixed population of Greeks and pagan Semites as well as Israelites, seeing the Roman debark from his vessel in the crowded harbor, could have provided the answer: "This land is holy, given by God, who made heaven and earth, to the people of Israel, whose seed and off-spring we are. It can be governed properly only by those to whom God has given it, not by pagans, whoever they may be, however noble their intentions. Nor can we admit Rome's intentions to be quite what the Romans claim. A century ago they came to settle a local struggle and somehow never found their way to the door. True enough, we have disagreements within our people. But only those whom Rome has bought deny the wrongness of Rome's rule among us. Indeed, some among us see the current age as drawing to an end. The coming one will dawn quite soon. Then will we be ruled by God's anointed as in days of old. Our former glory will be restored. When that day comes, all the good promises of the prophets of yore will come true. In the splendor of our coming king, we shall live in God's prosperity. Hosts of angels will do battle for us. None will make us afraid. Nations will come to Jerusalem for justice, as now they come to Rome."

Not all Romans were sober and high-principled, nor were all Jews vividly caught up in the messianic fervor of the age. But so many eagerly awaited the outbreak of the messianic dawn that Palestine proved ungovernable. No matter how scrupulously the Romans avoided offending the feelings of the tense and excitable populace, their very presence was the grandest offense. Their imminent departure through divine intervention seemed to some Jews to be perfectly certain. Had Palestine been situated in a less strategic place, had Rome concerned herself with the West alone, had the Jews modulated their hopes or directed them in other, less worldly paths, the encounter which in a very few years became a disastrous collision would have been avoided.

If that Caesarean Jew had lived to the year 66, he may well have died in the gentile reaction to the Jews' riots following the rout of a few Roman detachments in the hills. If that Roman soldier had remained in his Palestinian post, he may have fallen in a springtime ambush, or he may have survived to toss a burning torch onto the roof of the Temple's portico on an August day four years later. Roman and Jew alike would have judged the age to be drawing to a close, as indeed it was. To the Roman, as we have noted, Jewry had polluted its land "by its deeds and by its suffering." To the Jew, the Messiah must be very near at hand. To both, therefore, whatever might happen henceforward, the past had died and only awaited decent burial. In all that frenzied generation, Yoḥanan ben Zakkai alone had another perception of matters. It was he who before the war counseled caution in the manner of a sober Roman. Afterward he acted boldly to hold onto the past and preserve it.

PART ONE: CHAOS & ROUTINE
I. Faithful City, Faithful People

i. The Temple

From near and far pilgrims climbed the paths to Jerusalem. Distant lands sent their annual tribute, taxes imposed by a spiritual rather than a worldly sovereignty. Everywhere Jews turned to the Temple mountain when they prayed. Although Jews differed about matters of law and theology, the meaning of history and the timing of the Messiah's arrival, most affirmed the holiness of Ariel, Jerusalem, the faithful city. It was here that the sacred drama of the day must be enacted. And looking backward, we know they were right. It was indeed the fate of Jerusalem which in the end shaped the faith of Judaism for endless generations to come—but not quite in the ways that most men expected before A.D. 70.

How had Jerusalem cast its spell upon the Jews of far-off lands, to bring them together in their hearts' yearning? For centuries Israel had sung with the psalmist, "Our feet were standing within thy courts, O Jerusalem." They had exulted, "Pray for the peace of Jerusalem! May all prosper who seek your welfare!" Jews long contemplated the lessons of the old destruction. They were sure that by learning what Jeremiah, Ezekiel, and (Second) Isaiah taught about the meaning of the catastrophe of 586 B.C., by keeping the faith which prophecy demanded, they had ensured the city's eternity. Even then the Jews were a very old people. Their own records, translated into the language of all civilized men, testified to their antiquity. They could look back upon ancient enemies now forgotten by history, and ancient disasters, the spiritual lessons of which illumined current times. People thought that they kept the faith by devotion to the holy city, to the sacred Temple, to divinely ordained rites of service, to the priesthood, to the altar. And many a Jew yearned to see the priests upon their platform, to hear the Levites in their great choir singing the songs of David, to receive the blessing of the Lord in the Temple in Jerusalem. If people thought they kept the faith, they had good reason. What had the Lord commanded of old, which now they did not do? For three sins the ancient temple had fallen—murder, adultery, and idolatry. Now, five centuries later, idolatry was a grotesque memory. Murder and adultery were surely not so common among those whom God had instructed as elsewhere, they supposed. As to ancient Scriptures, were these not studied in the synagogues Sabbath upon Sabbath? But the most certain testimony of all to the enduring covenant was the Temple, which stood as the nexus between man and God. Its services bore witness to Israel's enduring loyalty to the covenant and the commandments of Sinai. They saw Jerusalem with the eye of faith, and that vision transformed the city.

We might see it as it was to appreciate the transforming power of faith. Even then, Herod's great project of beautifying and rebuilding the Temple was well under way. Throughout the first century, until the very eve of the war against Rome in 66, thousands of workmen busied themselves on the project. In the eighteenth year of his reign Herod had ordered plans drawn up to reconstruct the pile. It was to conform to the architecturally difficult dimensions of Solomon's temple, that is, sixty cubits long, twenty wide, and forty high. At the entrance of the outer temple hung a veil embroidered in blue, white, scarlet, and purple. The entry hall itself was divided from the Holy of Holies by a similar tapestry. The outer curtain was folded back on the south side and the inner one on the north, so that a priest entering the Holy of Holies crossed the court diagonally. At the gate were huge grape clusters. The building included side structures with space for three stories of chambers on the north, south, and west. East of the Temple, as in the time of Solomon, was a porch a hundred cubits wide, a hundred high, twenty deep, and a gateway. The front of the porch was gilded. When the rays of the morning sun fell on it, the glow illumined the city and could be seen from a great distance. In front of the Temple stood the altar for burnt offerings. To the north twenty-four rings were fixed to the ground, to which sacrificial animals were tied. Nearby, eight pillars supported cedar beams, on which the carcasses of animals were hung. Eight marble tables for preparing the flesh and a bronze laver for priestly ablutions were provided. Herod had greatly expanded the temple area and sloped the sides of the mountain steeply so that the building would look taller than it actually was. The whole he surrounded by a massive wall. Between the valley and the city was a causeway. The Temple courts were paved in mosaics or white marble, with numerous columns, and the ceilings were carved wood. The outer court was not part of the Temple, and its soil was not sacred. Anyone might come in. But non-Jews were warned not to proceed farther. Women might go past the court of the gentiles into an inner court. Only men might go into the Temple proper, and only priests into certain precincts. So much for the building.

The activity was endless. Priests hurried to and fro, important because of their tribe, sacred because of their task, officiating at the sacrifices morning and eventide, busying themselves through the day with the Temple's needs. They were always careful to keep the levitical rules of purity which God decreed, they thought, for just this place and hour. Levites assisting them and responsible for the public liturgies could be seen everywhere. In the outer courts Jews from all parts of the world, speaking many languages, changed their foreign money for the Temple coin. They brought up their sheqel, together with the freewill, or peace, or sin, or other offerings they were liable to give. Outside, in the city beyond, craftsmen created the necessary vessels or repaired broken ones. Incense makers mixed spices. Animal-dealers selected the most perfect beasts. In the schools young priests were taught the ancient law, to which in time they would conform as had their ancestors before them, exactly as did their fathers that very day. All the population either directly or indirectly was engaged in some way in the work of the Temple. The city lived for it, by it, and on its revenues. In modern terms, Jerusalem was a center of pilgrimage, and its economy was based upon tourism.

But no one saw things in such a light. Jerusalem had an industry, to be sure, but if a Jew were asked, "What is the business of this city?" he would have replied without guile, "It is a holy city, and its work is the service of God on high." Only a few men doubted it. For reasons of their own, those who formed the commune at the Dead Sea abandoned the Temple, regarding it as hopelessly impure, its calendar as erroneous. Others, the Pharisees, thought that the priests should conduct themselves in accordance with the oral tradition they believed God had revealed to Moses at Sinai, that Moses had transmitted to the prophets, and the prophets to sages, down to that very day and to their own group. But even they were among the Temple's loyal servants. The Temple was the center of the world. They said the mount was the highest hill in the world. To it in time would come the anointed of God. In the meantime, they taught, the Temple sacrifice was the way to serve God, a way he, himself, in remotest times had decreed. True, there were other ways believed to be more important, for the prophets had emphasized that sacrifice alone was not enough to reconcile the sinner to a God made angry by unethical or immoral behavior. Morality, ethics, humility, good faith—these, too, he required. But good faith meant loyalty to the covenant which had specified, among other things, that the priests do just what they were doing. The animal sacrifices, the incense, the oil, wine, and bread were to be arrayed in the service of the Most High.

ii. *"Because of Their Sins"*

Later, men condemned this generation. Christians and Jews alike reflected upon the destruction of the great sanctuary. They looked to the alleged misdeeds of those who lived at the time for reasons to account for the destruction. No generation in the history of Jewry has been so roundly, universally condemned by posterity as that of Yoḥanan ben Zakkai. Christians remembered, in the tradition of the Church, that Jesus wept over the city and said a bitter, sorrowing sentence:

> O Jerusalem, Jerusalem, killing the prophets and stoning those who are sent to you! How often would I have gathered your children together as a hen gathers her brood under her wings, and you would not! Behold, your house is forsaken and desolate. For I tell you, you will not see me again, until you say, "Blessed is he who comes in the name of the Lord." (Matt. 23:37-39)

And when the disciples pointed out the Temple buildings from a distance, he said to them, "You see all these, do you not? Truly, I say to you, there will not be left here one stone upon another, that will not be thrown down." (Matt. 24:2; cf. Luke 21:6.) So for twenty centuries, Jerusalem was seen through the eye of Christian faith as a faithless city, killing prophets, and therefore desolated by the righteous act of a wrathful God.

But Jews said no less. From the time of the destruction, they prayed: "On account of our sins we have been exiled from our land, and we have been removed far from our country. We cannot go up to appear and bow down before you, to carry out our duties in your chosen Sanctuary, in the great and holy house upon which your name was called." It is not a great step from "our sins," to "the sins of the generation in whose time the Temple was destroyed." It is not a difficult conclusion, and not a few have reached it. The Temple was destroyed mainly because of the sins of the Jews of that time, particularly "causeless hatred." Whether the sins were those specified by Christians or by Talmudic rabbis hardly matters. This was supposed to be a sinning generation.

It was *not* a sinning generation, but one deeply faithful to the covenant and to the Scripture that set forth its terms, perhaps more so than many who have since condemned it. Yoḥanan's contemporaries sinned only by their failure. Had they overcome Rome, even in the circles of the rabbis they

25

would have found high praise, for success indicates the will of Providence. But on what grounds are they to be judged sinners? The Temple was destroyed, but it was destroyed because of a brave and courageous, if hopeless war. That war was waged not for the glory of a king or for the aggrandizement of a people, but in the hope that at its successful conclusion, pagan rule would be extirpated from the holy land. This was the articulated motive. It was a war fought explicitly for the sake and in the name of God. The struggle called forth prophets and holy men, leaders whom the people did not kill or stone, but courageously followed past all hope of success. Jews were not demoralized or cowardly, afraid to die because they had no faith in what they were doing, fearful to dare because they did not want to take risks. The Jerusalemites fought with amazing courage, despite unbelievable odds. Since they lost, later generations looked for their sin, for none could believe that the omnipotent God would permit his Temple to be destroyed for no reason. As after 586 B.C., so after 70, the alternative was this: "Either our fathers greatly sinned, or God is not just." The choice thus represented no choice at all. "God is just, but we have sinned—we, but mostly our fathers before us. Therefore, all that has come upon us—the famine, the exile, the slavery to pagans—these are just recompense for our own deeds."

iii. Zakkai

Since Yoḥanan died shortly after the destruction of Jerusalem, possibly about the year 80, and was credited with extraordinary longevity, he probably was born soon after the end of the reign of Herod the Great, at about the beginning of the common era. Who was this Zakkai, who named his son Yoḥanan (John), "the Lord gave graciously"? The sources do not say. The sole shred of information is the name *Zakkai* itself. *Zakkai* was the Aramaic equivalent of the Hebrew *ẓaddiq*, righteous, upright. This much is clear from the Aramaic translation of Scripture, for in Genesis 6:9, the Hebrew reads, "These are the generations of Noah. Noah was a *righteous man,* blameless in his generation." The Aramaic translator used the word *zakkai.* It was also the name of a clan that returned from Babylon. Listed among those who came back to Judah were "the sons of Zakkai, seven hundred and sixty" (Ezra 2:9, Nehemiah 7:14). The sons of Zakkai were a clan of commoners, "the men of the people of Israel." They were not among those distinguished as priests, Levites, Temple servants, sons of Solomon's servants, singers, or gatekeepers. Yet the clan amounted to something. In a group of less than forty-five thousand, a family of more than seven hundred fifty members must have been prominent.

Others named Zakkai appear again in rabbinic literature. Rabbi Zakkai, a tanna, was contemporary of Judah the Prince (ca. A.D. 200), and a Babylonian Amora of the third century, R. Zakkai, was known to have emigrated to the land of Israel, where he became chief lecturer at one of the leading academies, and was called "the Babylonian." Otherwise, however, the name does not occur. If we wanted to translate "Yoḥanan ben Zakkai" into English, it would come out "John the Righteous."

iv. Herod

Yoḥanan's father had witnessed much of Herod's reign. Herod had hoped to build a realm for the dynasty he founded and had allied himself with Rome. It was imperial policy in Herod's time to exert authority through territorial monarchs, petty kings who ruled frontier territories still too unruly to receive a Roman viceroy. Rome later came to govern the protectorates through her own agents. She finally incorporated the subjugated lands into the normal provincial structure. Thus in Armenia, Cilicia, and other territories on the Parthian frontier, Rome established or supported friendly kings, ethnarchs, and tetrarchs, thereby governing through subservient agents in lands where she herself did not choose to rule. Honored by Rome with the titles *Socius et Amicus Populi Romani,* "associate and friend of Roman people," and, in the East, *Philo-Romaios* and *Philo-Kaiser,* "friend of

Rome," "friend of Caesar," Herod governed efficiently. He collected revenues, contrived public works to develop vast tracts of land and eliminate unemployment, and, as we have seen, constructed a magnificent temple in Jerusalem. He also built several large cities, fortresses, and palaces including Herodion in the south, Sebaste in Samaria, and Caesarea, a seaport in the Sharon. Herod stabilized political life, which had been in turmoil during the reign of the last Hasmonean monarchs. Indeed, under him there were no politics at all, only palace intrigue and slaughter of potentially dangerous wives, sons, and servants. Most Jews simply could not participate in public affairs. Many retired from the stage of political history. Earlier institutions of political life were either transformed into instruments of state, like the high priesthood, or apparently ignored, like the Sanhedrin. Under Herod, official culture came more and more under Hellenistic domination. Court history was written in Greek by able Syrians. The Temple cult was managed by agents of the monarchy, men who purchased the high priesthood at a price, held it at the king's pleasure, and, enriched by the priestly dues, handed it in the accepted Greek manner to the next appointee. It was a brilliant reign, but in the wrong time and over the wrong people.

After Herod's death in 6 B.C., the people begged for direct Roman government. "They implored the Romans to unite their country to Syria and to entrust its administration to Roman governors. The Jews would then show that, though people said they were factious and always at war, they knew how to obey equitable rulers." The Romans tried to keep Herod's sons in power, but when this led to further difficulties, they acquiesced and appointed the first in a line of procurators. The procurators did not share Herod's interest in developing the economy by building port cities and roads. They were mainly concerned with the imperial welfare, if not, first of all, with their own. They lived in Hellenistic Caesarea, went up to Jerusalem when masses of pilgrims came up to celebrate the festivals, and were glad to return to the cosmopolitan capital as soon as possible. When, in the spring of A.D. 66, one of them, Cestius, did not survive a bloody ambush on the road back, the revolution began. Then procuratorial government ended as abruptly as it had begun.

v. Economic Life

The first act of procuratorial government was normally to divide the conquered territory into municipal districts; the second was to take a census, determining the rate at which cities could be expected to contribute to the treasury. Taxes were applied to men, houses, animals, sales, imports, and exports (at a moderate rate) and were collected by an efficient bureaucracy. Besides these taxes Jews paid dues to another sovereignty as well, that imposed by the ancestral faith. The Bible had detailed many kinds of priestly and Levitical offerings and animal sacrifices to support the expensive Temple cult. Under a priestly government these taxes would certainly have supported a large administration. This doubtless was the economic rationale for the multitudinous tithes and offerings. Although the priests had ceased to rule, they still claimed their dues. With Roman help they obtained some of them from the majority of Jews and all from the very pious. Throughout these years Jews thus were paying a twofold tax. The extent of civil and religious taxation has been estimated at from thirty to forty per cent of the gross national income, but it was probably considerably lower since the majority of the Jews paid only a small part of the religious imposts.

In any event the Jews never regarded Roman rule as legitimate. Taxes were therefore seen to be robbery. The Pharisaic sages made no distinction between a tax collector and a thief or an extortioner. As Louis Ginzberg pointed out, the sages regarded gentile rulers in Palestine as robbers, without any rights whatsoever either in the land or over its inhabitants. No pagan power whatever had any right in the land. No land acquisition could free a field user from the obligation to pay the tithes. Even if a gentile bought land from a Jew, he was held to be a sharecropper. No gentile could ever take valid, legal possession of any part of the land. This attitude to the rightful ownership of the land affected collection of taxes and much else, as we shall see. But religious imposts were something else again. The Pharisees believed they must be paid. Pharisees therefore separated themselves from Jews who neglected the tithes and heave-offerings or paid only part of them. It was one of the main distinctions between the Pharisaic masters and disciples, on the one hand, and the common people on the other. The former were meticulous in paying the priestly and Levitical dues, and the latter were not.

Roman rule was advantageous for some. It opened the way for adventurous men to undertake vast enterprises in commerce and travel. Many took advantage of the opportunities of the Roman Empire to move to more prosperous lands. Throughout this period one discovers Jews settling in the most remote corners of the empire and beyond. Those who stayed at home benefited from economic stability. Among them was Yoḥanan ben Zakkai. One source records that he was a tradesman. "One hundred and twenty years he lived. Forty years he spent in business, forty years he studied, and forty years he sustained all Israel." Precisely when he was in business we do not know. This, like the circumstances of his birth, does not receive illumination even from legend. If he made his living in some urban trade, he enjoyed the advantage of the stable currency which Rome introduced. The land did not produce precious metals. It thus had to depend on foreign coinage for most of its currency. The value of the currency depended on external factors. It might be withdrawn or debased without warning. Its purchasing power might diminish in the fluctuation of foreign commodity markets. The Romans, holding the right to make copper, silver, and gold coins, incorporated the land into the advanced economy of the eastern Mediterranean. They made possible extensive exploitation of the trade opportunities there. Situated on the trade routes to the east and south, the coastal cities, which contained large Jewish minorities, imported new wares for sale in the bazaars and markets of back country towns like Jerusalem. The Jewish economy in the land flourished. Roman peace, Herodian enterprise, the natural endowments of the land, and broad economic opportunities combined to yield an adequate subsistence in a relatively stable economy for a very large population.

Living standards nonetheless were modest. Archaeologists have not turned up pretentious synagogues, treasures of gems, rich pottery, furnishings, or costly sarcophagi dating from the first century. Life was simple. People ate cheap foods such as salted fish, bread made from low grades of local wheat, low-quality grain imported from Egypt, or barley. They drank beer or wine diluted with water and sweetened their food with honey. Meat was eaten mostly on festival occasions, fish on the Sabbath. Judea was famed for its date palms, and the palm tree was sometimes engraved on coins as the emblem of the land. Most men lived by farming or handicrafts. Contemporary parables borrow the imagery of fishing, agriculture, and petty trade. Few related to large-scale commerce. Riches meant a long-term food supply or a good wife. No parables refer to sophisticated problems of government, but many allude to a majestic, exalted monarch much magnified from the viewpoint of the mute populace.

One piece of evidence indicates that Yoḥanan did know the intricacies of small business. He was well informed about how men falsify weights and measures. A discussion took place on what constitutes an object susceptible to uncleanness, that is, an object which has a receptacle, such as a walking stick with a secret compartment or the beam of a balance or a leveling rod with a hidden receptacle to receive false weights. Was such an object susceptible on that account to uncleanness? So too, was a carrying yoke with a secret receptacle for money or a stick with a secret place for pearls considered a legitimate vessel? All of these questionable devices by which men might cheat one another were declared capable of becoming unclean. Concerning all of them Yoḥanan said, "Woe is me if I speak, woe is me if I do not! If I speak, I may teach the deceivers how to cheat. But if I do not, the deceivers will say that the disciples of the sages do not know about our schemes."

vi. Education

After the educational reforms of the first century B.C. many of the people, rich and poor alike, received an education in the main disciplines of Jewish tradition. This education, centering on religious learning, was sufficiently broad to impart civilizing and humanizing lessons. What did ordinary people study? They learned the Holy Scriptures. They, therefore, considered the history of the world from creation onward. They were taught in lessons about their forefathers, Abraham, Isaac, and Jacob, to emulate patriarchal hospitality to men and faithfulness to God. They studied about the life and laws of Moses. From those laws they gained an idea of how a covenanted community should conduct its affairs. They were instructed about their obligations to the poor, weak, orphaned, homeless, the stranger, and the outsider. They were educated to say that God is one, and that there are no other gods. They were told about the prophets whom God had sent to warn before ancient disasters and to exhort afterward. Those prophets had said that what God wanted of man was that he do justice, love mercy, and walk humbly before God. The people learned that Providence guided their fate and that nothing happened but that God decreed it. So they were taught to look for the meaning of daily and cosmic events alike. A comet, drought, broken leg, or earthquake—all could equally convey a truth. In the biblical writings they studied the wisdom of ancient sages, learning prudence, piety, and understanding.

In modern terms their curriculum included much attention to matters of metaphysics, law and morality, ethics and history. Such lessons were intended to create a decent human being. Perhaps everyday conduct revealed something of their impact but it was the historical lesson that seems to have had the greatest effect. God had given the land to Israel. Pagans had held it for a time, because in ancient days the people had sinned. But Israel had gotten it back after God had purified the people through suffering. In time, God again would set things straight and send a king like David of old, anointed in the manner of the ancient monarchy, to sit upon Mount Zion and dispense justice and revelation to all nations.

vii. Social Classes

Class divisions were complicated by the regional variations of the land. Jerusalem was the metropolis of the Jews. Its populace included a significant number of wealthy men, both absentee landlords and great merchants, as well as many priests who lived on the priestly dues and Temple endowments. The city also contained a smaller class of Levites, who performed certain nonsacrificial tasks in the sanctuary and managed the buildings. Artisans whose skills were indispensable in the building and maintenance of the Temple, petty traders, a large urban proletariat, and unskilled laborers filled the crowded streets. Jerusalemites tended to separate themselves from the Judean provincials for both social and ritual reasons. Living in close proximity to the sanctuary, the men of the city were more concerned about observing the requirements of ritual cleanness, imposed by residence in the holy place, than were the provincials who purified themselves mainly for the festal pilgrimages. The provincials often did not have the benefit of much advanced education. Animosities between urban and rural residents were bitter. The provincials themselves were by no means united. The country gentry, landowners holding considerable property in the fertile lowland plains, had less in common with their highland neighbors than with the urban upper bourgeoisie.

On the other hand, the rural farmers and proletariat submerged classes, were divorced from the main issues of national life. They welcomed the ministry of powerful personalities, sometimes sages empowered by learning, but more often wonder-workers able to heal mind and body. Jericho and the Southern Plain were the main centers of the rural gentility. On the rocky Judean hills lived the rural yeomen and proletariat. In Galilee class divisions between wealthier and poorer peasants likewise were manifest. Hundreds of rural villages, large and small, clustered in the fertile hills and valleys of the north. Only Sepphoris and Tiberias were large urban centers, and they did not dominate the province as Jerusalem did Judea.

viii. The Sects: Essenes, Sadducees, Pharisees

The main social and religious events of this period held little interest for contemporary historians. Josephus, for one, paid very little attention to the inner life of Israel in his rich narrative of politics and war. His histories provide evidence that the masses of men had turned away from public affairs. They may have responded to changes in their political situation. They may have felt growing impatience with social inequity or with the alien government whose benefits were not obvious to them. Only in the riots and continuous unrest toward the end of this period, however, does their response become entirely evident. A few indicated their disapproval of the course of events by withdrawing from the common society. Some became hermits; some fled to other lands or entered monastic communities in which contact with the outside world was minimal.

The monastic commune near the shores of the Dead Sea was one such group. To the barren heights came men seeking purity and hoping for eternity. The purity they sought was not from common dirt, but from the uncleanness of this world, symbolized by contact with the impure insects or objects Scripture had declared unclean. In their minds that uncleanness carried a far deeper meaning. This age was impure and therefore would soon be coming to an end. Those who wanted to do the Lord's service should prepare themselves for a holy war at the end of time. The commune at the Dead Sea, therefore, divided by ranks under captains lived under military discipline and studied the well-known holy books as well as books other men did not know about. These books specified when and how the holy war would be fought and the manner of life of those worthy to fight it. Men and women came to Qumran with their property, which they contributed to the common fund. There they prepared for a fateful day, not too long to be postponed, scarcely looking backward at those remaining in the corruption of this world. These Jews would be the last, smallest, "saving remnant" of all. Yet through them all mankind would come to know the truth. They prepared for Armeggedon and their battle against forces of ritual impurity, evil and sin alike, was for the Lord. The Qumran commune ordained: "This is the regulation for the men of the commune, who devote themselves to turn away from all evil, and to hold fast to all that he has commanded as his will, to separate themselves from the congregation of men of iniquity to be a commune in Torah and property." Likewise the psalmist of Qumran prayed:

> Only as you draw a man near will I love him.
> And as you keep him far away, so will I abominate him.

The members of wilderness communes described by Philo as Essenes avoided the settled society of town and city, "because of the inequities which have become inveterate among city dwellers, for they know that their company would have a deadly effect upon their own souls." The communards sanctified themselves by meticulous observance of the rules of ritual purity and tried to found such a society as they thought worthy of receiving God's approval. Strikingly, they held that God, himself, had revealed to Moses the very laws they now obeyed.

Pharisees, probably meaning Separatists, also believed that all was not in order with the world, but they chose another way, likewise attributed to Mosaic legislation. They remained within the common society in accordance with the teaching of Hillel, "Do not separate yourself from the community." The Pharisaic community therefore sought to rebuild society on its own ruins with its own mortar and brick. They differed among themselves. Some, called Zealots, accepted the Pharisaic interpretation of tradition, but thought to restore the fortune of Israel through war. Others focused their efforts in the spiritual reform of the nation. The Pharisees actively fostered their opinions on tradition and religion among the whole people. According to Josephus, "They are able greatly to influence the masses of the people. Whatever the people do about divine worship, prayers, and sacrifices, they perform according to their direction. The cities give great praise to them on account of their virtuous conduct, both in the actions of their lives and their teachings also." Though Josephus exaggerated the extent of their power, the Pharisees certainly exerted some influence in the religious life of Israel before they finally came to power in 70.

Among the men sympathetic to the Pharisaic cause were some who entered into an urban religious communion, a mostly unorganized society known as the fellowship (*ḥavurah*). The basis of this society was meticulous observance of laws of tithing and other priestly offerings as well as the rules of ritual purity outside the Temple where they were not mandatory. The members undertook to eat even profane foods (not sacred tithes or other offerings) in a state of rigorous levitical cleanness. At table, they compared themselves to Temple priests at the altar. These rules tended to segregate the members of the fellowship, for they ate only with those who kept the law as they thought proper. The fellows thus mediated between the obligation to observe religious precepts and the injunction to remain within the common society. By keeping the rules of purity the fellow separated from the common man, but by remaining within the towns and cities of the land, he preserved the possibility of teaching others by example. The fellows lived among, but not with, the people of the land. With neither formal structure nor officers and bylaws as at Qumran, the fellowship represented the polity of people who recognized one another as part of the same inchoate community. They formed a new, if limited, society within the old. They were the few who kept what they held to be the faith in the company of the many who did not.

Upper class opinion was expressed in the viewpoint of still another group, the Sadducees. They stood for strict adherence to the written word in religious matters, conservatism in both ritual and belief. Their name probably derived from the priesthood of Ẓaddoq, established by David ten centuries earlier. They differed from the Pharisees especially on the doctrine of revelation. They acknowledged Scripture as the only authority, themselves as its sole arbiters. They denied that its meaning might be elucidated by the Pharisees' allegedly ancient traditions attributed to Moses or by the Pharisaic devices of exegesis and scholarship. The Pharisees claimed that Scripture and the traditional oral interpretation were one. To the Sadducees such a claim of unity was spurious and masked innovation. They differed also on the eternity of the soul. The Pharisees believed in the survival of the soul, the revival of the body, the day of judgment, and life in the world to come. The Sadducees found nothing in Scripture which to their way of thinking supported such doctrines. They ridiculed both these ideas and the exegesis which made them possible. They won over the main body of officiating priests and wealthier men. With the destruction of the Temple their ranks were decimated. Very little literature later remained to preserve their viewpoint. It is difficult indeed to compare them to the other sects. They may have constituted no social institution like the Pharisaic and Essenic groups. In their day, however, the Sadducees claimed to be the legitimate heirs of Israel's faith. Holding positions of power and authority, they succeeded in leaving so deep an impression on society that even their Pharisaic, Essenic, and Christian opponents did not wholly wipe out their memory.

The Sadducees were most influential among landholders and merchants, the Pharisees among the middle and lower urban classes, the Essenes among the disenchanted of both these classes. These classes and sectarian divisions manifested a vigorous inner life, with politics revolving about peculiarly Jewish issues such as matters of exegesis, law, doctrine, and the meaning of history. The vitality of Israel would have astonished the Roman administration, and when it burst forth, it did.

ix. Conversion

The rich variety of Jewish religious expression in this period ought not to obscure the fact that for much of Jewish Palestine, Judaism was a relatively new phenomenon. Herod was the grandson of pagans. Similarly, the entire Galilee had been converted to Judaism only one hundred and twenty years before the Common Era. In the later expansion of the Hasmonean kingdom, other regions were forcibly brought within the fold. The Hasmoneans used Judaism imperially, as a means of winning the loyalty of the pagan Semites in the regions of Palestine they conquered. But in a brief period of three or four generations the deeply-rooted practices of the Semitic natives of Galilee, Idumea, and other areas could not have been wiped out. They were rather covered over with a veneer of monotheism. Hence the newly converted territories, though vigorously loyal to their new faith, were no more Judaized in so short a time than were the later Russians, Poles, Celts, or Saxons Christianized within a century.

It took a great effort to transform an act of circumcision of the flesh, joined with a mere verbal affirmation of one God, done under severe duress, into a deepening commitment to faith. And yet in the war of 66 the Jews of newly converted regions fought with great loyalty. While the Galileans had proved unable to stand upon the open battlefield, many of them together with Idumeans retreated to the holy city. There they gave their lives in the last great cataclysms of the war. The exceptional loyalty of the newly converted regions would lead one to suppose that it was to the Temple cult, to the God whom it served, and to the nation which supported it, that the pagan Semites were originally converted. They could have known little of the more difficult service of the heart through study of Torah and ethical and moral action which the Pharisees demanded.

While the central teachings of the faith were very ancient, adherence of many who professed it was therefore only relatively recent and superficial. The Pharisaic party, dating at least from the second century B.C., if not much earlier, never solidly established itself in Galilee before the second century A.D. The religious beliefs of recently converted people could not have encompassed ideas and issues requiring substantial study, elaborate schooling, and a well-established pattern of

living. Conversion of one group to another faith never obliter-
ates the former culture, but rather entails the translation of the
new into the idiom of the old, so that in the end it results in a
modification of both. The newly Judaized regions similarly
must have preserved substantial remnants of their former
pagan Semitic and Hellenistic culture. The inhabitants could
not have been greatly changed merely by receiving "Judaism,"
which meant in the beginning little more than submitting to
the knife of the circumcizer rather than to the sword of the
slaughterer. Only after many generations was the full implica-
tion of conversion realized in the lives of the people in Galilee, and then mainly because great centers of Tannaitic law
and teaching were established among them.

For this period, however, no such thing as "normative Judaism" existed, from which one or another "heretical" group
might diverge. Not only in the great center of the faith, Jerusalem, do we find numerous competing groups, but throughout the country and abroad we may discern a religious tradition in the midst of great flux. It was full of vitality, but in the
end without a clear and widely accepted view of what was required of each man, apart from acceptance of Mosaic revelation. And this could mean whatever you wanted. People would
ask one teacher after another, "What must I do to enter the
kingdom of heaven," precisely because no authoritative answer existed. In the end two groups emerged, the Christians
and the rabbis, heirs of the Pharisaic sages. Each offered an
all-encompassing interpretation of Scripture, explaining what
it did and did not mean. Each promised salvation for individ-
uals and for Israel as a whole. Of the two, the rabbis achieved
somewhat greater success among the Jews. Wherever
the rabbis' views of Scripture were propagated the Christian
view of the meaning of biblical, especially prophetic, revelation and its fulfillment made relatively little progress. This
was true, specifically, in Jewish Palestine itself, certain cities
in Mesopotamia, and in central Babylonia. Where the rabbis
were not to be found, as in Egyptian Alexandria, Syria, Asia
Minor, Greece, and in the west, Christian biblical interpretation and salvation through Christ risen from the dead found

a ready audience among the Jews. It was not without good reason that the gospel tradition of Matthew saw in the "scribes and Pharisees" the chief opponents of Jesus' ministry. Whatever the historical facts of that ministry, the rabbis proved afterward to be the greatest stumbling block for the Christian mission to the Jews.

x. Self-Government

It was a peculiar circumstance of Roman imperial policy that facilitated the growth of such a vigorous inner life and permitted the development of nonpolitical institutions to express it. Rome carefully respected Jewish rights to limited self-government. The populace was subject to its own law and quarrels were adjudicated by its own judges. Rome had specific and clearly defined purposes for the empire. Her policies could be adequately effected without totalitarian interference into the inner affairs of the conquered peoples. The same indifference to local sensitivities that very occasionally permitted a procurator to bring his military standards into a city pure of "graven images" likewise encouraged him to ignore territorial affairs of considerable weight.

The national tribunal, called variously the Sanhedrin or High Court, acted with a measure of freedom to determine internal policy in religion, ritual, cult, and local law. The Sanhedrin lost authority to inflict capital punishment, it is generally assumed, shortly after Judea became a part of the Syrian provincial administration. Whether, in fact, it had administered the death penalty in Herod's reign is not entirely clear. The court certainly maintained the right to direct Temple affairs. It decided matters of civil and commercial law and torts and defined personal and family status and marriage procedure. The court also collected the biblical levies and determined the sacred calendar. It thus represented the one abiding institutional expression of Israel's inner autonomy during the procuratorial regime. Both the Pharisees and Sadducees took an active interest in the religious, social, and economic administration of Israel's life. The Sanhedrin provided a means to formulate and effect these interests. The leaders of both major viewpoints played a considerable part in the nation's autonomous affairs. The exact nature of Jewish self-government and the institutions that embodied it has not yet been finally clarified. The sources are difficult; no body of sources presents a picture that can be wholly verified in some other independent tradition. It seems to me the most likely view for the present is that of Professor E. E. Urbach:

> The theories that posit the existence of two Courts (a civil Sanhedrin, over which the High Priests presided, and a religious court, at the head of which stood the Patriarchs and Presidents of the Court) are supported neither by the literary sources nor by the historic reality. There was only one Sanhedrin, the one that met in the Hewn Chamber. . . . The Sanhedrin adjoined the altar . . . . It was a court composed of "priests, Levites and Israelites who may give their daughters in marriage to priests. . . . The High Priest was permitted to preside at the Sanhedrin. . . . Throughout its existence the institution was enveloped by an aura of sanctity and supreme authority, and just as the holiness of the Temple was not impaired in the estimation of the Sages by the High Priests who were unworthy of officiating, so it never entered their minds to repudiate the institution of the Sanhedrin or to set up a rival to it in the form of a competing court. They endeavored rather to exercise their influence and to introduce their rulings and views even into the ritual of the Temple service and into the Sanhedrin's methods of operation. They did not always enjoy success, and not infrequently clashed with High Priests as well as with other bureaucrats and office-holders.

One of the Pharisaic leaders, in many ways the most important, was Hillel the Elder who, with his colleague Shammai, recieved the "Torah" from Shemaiah and Avtalion and handed it on, according to the Pharisaic chain of tradition, to Yoḥanan ben Zakkai. Urbach notes, however, that "there is no proof that R. Yoḥanan held any office whatsoever when he was in Jerusalem."

xi. Conclusion

Yohanan ben Zakkai came into a world of irrepressible conflict. That conflict was between two pieties, two universal conceptions of what the world required. On the one hand, the Roman imperialist thought that good government, that is, Roman government, must serve to keep the peace. Rome would bring the blessings of civil order and material progress to many lands. For the Roman that particular stretch of hills, farmland, and desert that Jews called "the Land of Israel" meant little economically, but a great deal strategically. No wealth could be hoped for, but to lose Palestine would mean to lose the keystone of empire in the east. We see Palestine from the perspective of the west. It appears as a land bridge between Egypt and Asia Minor, the corner of a major trade route. But to the imperial strategist, Palestine loomed as the bulwark of the eastern frontier against Parthia. The Parthians, holding the Tigris-Euphrates frontier, were a mere few hundred miles from Palestine, separated by a desert no one could control. If the Parthians could take Palestine, Egypt would fall into their hand. Parthian armies moreover were pointed like a sword toward Antioch and the seat of empire established there. Less than a century earlier they had actually captured Jerusalem and seated upon its throne a puppet of their own. (That he was a Hasmonean meant less than that he might support the Parthians while controlling the people.) For a time they thrust Roman rule out of the eastern shores of the Mediterranean.

For Rome, therefore, Palestine was too close to the most dangerous frontier of all to be given up. Indeed, among all the Roman frontiers only the oriental one was now contested by a civilized and dangerous foe. Palestine lay behind the very lines upon which that enemy had to be met. Rome could ill afford such a loss. Egypt, moreover, was her granary, the foundation of her social welfare and wealth. The grain of Egypt sustained the masses of Rome herself. Economic and military considerations thus absolutely required the retention of Palestine. Had Palestine stood in a less strategic locale, matters might have been different. Rome had a second such frontier-territory to consider—Armenia. While she fought vigorously to retain predominance over the northern gateway to the Middle East, she generally remained willing to compromise on joint suzerainty with Parthia in Armenia—but not in Palestine.

For the Jew, Palestine meant something of even greater import. He believed that history depended upon what happened in the Land of Israel. He thought that from creation to end of time the events that took place in Jerusalem would shape the fate of all mankind. His, no less than Rome's, was an imperial view of the world, but with this difference: the empire was God's. If Rome could not lose Palestine, the Jew was unwilling to give it up. Rome scrupulously would do everything possible to please Jewry, permitting the Jews to keep their laws in exchange only for peaceful acquiescence to Roman rule. There was, alas, nothing Rome could actually do to please Jewry but evacuate Palestine. No amiable tolerance of local custom could suffice to win the people's submission.

Among irreconcilable contending forces one wonders how it was that Yoḥanan saw things otherwise. He took the stand that Rome was right, but not for her reasons. Israel was also to be justified, but only by God's ways. He was obsessed with peace in a time of war. In an age of force he believed in man's capacity freely to serve and love his neighbor. He had a different view of what God's rule must mean, of where God's rule must take place. No less than other Jews he regretted that Rome ruled in Palestine, but he thought the way forward lay not through the battlefield. God's dominion transcended the world. Whoever might rule below mattered less than who should rule within—and that issue would be decided, not by the sword but by the Torah. If Yoḥanan urged another way than war, it was because he had in mind different weapons, another battlefield. Until his very old age no one could have known that he was right. Nothing ever happened to suggest to him that others were wrong.

Yoḥanan's was the hardest fight of all. He had to struggle to keep the faith with his own mature vision of truth when all testified against it. Most of the great men of his time, Roman and Jewish alike, turned their backs on him. No man ever faced a lonelier or a more uncertain life. He was thought by the leaders of his own people to be a traitor, a coward, worst of all, a fool. He was received by the enemy as a useful collaborator, a quisling to be exploited, then discarded when no longer found convenient. From what source could he derive courage to speak despite the perverse certainty of crowds and the call of cynical generals? Upon whom could he lean in an age when men depended upon the sword and pursued violent visions? The story of his early years and education provides the answer.

II. Filling Their Treasuries

i. The Obscure Years

Where Yohanan came from no one knows. We know little about his early training. Since he entered the school of Hillel, one of the two great Pharisaic academies of the day, we may imagine that Yohanan had already distinguished himself in studies. Not everyone who finished the lower schools and studied Scripture and prayers, traditions and lore, ended up in the senior academy. Most went on to other tasks, trained in what they needed to know in order to live in accordance with Israel's tradition. Few were equipped to add to or reshape the tradition for the future. Let us suppose that Yohanan was not a Jerusalemite to begin with. Like his student Eliezer ben Hyrcanus, of whom we shall hear more later, he must have parted from his family home and his village. He would have known almost everyone at home. The streets and the fields would have been his familiar world. Had he stayed, he would have become a locally famous man. His learning already had set him apart for distinction. But even from his youth he must have had the sense that he would walk another path and spend his life among strangers. His was a call to a greater stage and to a larger role than that of village authority.

As he climbed up to the great city, this time alone and not on a Temple pilgrimage with his family, his heart must have ached. Behind lay all he loved; before, an unknown life. In Hillel's school he would be the least. None would know him. At home he had been known and admired by all. How many were his equal, but did not take his chance or came to school, but soon returned home? How many lasted only a little

while and then honestly reckoned with their real talent and
found it insufficient? The young and hopeful came from all
parts of the country to sit at the feet of the greatest men of
their people in the holiest place, working in Torah, the most
sacred pursuit of all. Among them, perhaps after the holy
season had ended and the time of studies began with the advent of the winter rains, a young man passed through the gates
of the city and entered the paths of learning. He would have
taken his place at the very back among the newcomers and
stayed there for a long time. These must have been times of
contentment, years of promise. Earlier he had outpaced his
fellow students. Even his village-teachers could not have
proved equal to the task of his education. Now he learned
from one and all, from the excited conversation of older students, from his masters at study. He also studied the life of
the streets which conformed to ancient laws not observed
elsewhere. He followed the precise cult of the Temple. The
sun rose and the city awoke to the knowledge that in its midst
God was served as nowhere else. It set and the smoke of the
offerings and the incense ascended. The resounding song of
the Levites echoed from hill to hill. To live in Jerusalem and
breathe its air was to grow in Torah.

The life of the young man not yet burdened with the responsibilities of the world must have been indeed serene. Yohanan did not have to struggle to realize among men what
the sages taught. The work of learning without the task of
doing proved sweet. As he sat in the freedom of his youth, not
yet called to go out to serve, he knew a peace that can be found
only in the "war of the Torah." He enjoyed happiness known
only to those who are its stalwart warriors. The wars, the
struggles of those years were the best kind. They were wars of
truth with truth's protagonist. They imposed the struggle to
learn by memory and by reason. The battle was to overcome
the flesh's sloth and the mind's recalcitrance, but not the
world's hostility.

It was the wisdom of the Pharisaic masters to discern that
mastery of all other struggles would depend upon that first
and greatest—the overcoming of one's lesser impulses. The

masters stressed "Torah," which meant the act of learning what the former generations of their group had believed God told Moses to pass on in oral tradition. They thus ensured that everyone who came out of their academies with the mark of their approval would have faced and overcome the greatest enemy of all—the self. It was, after all, the natural desire of young men to look for easy distinction. The rabbis prevented it by insisting that true achievement depended upon depth of learning and not upon the early experience of public responsibility. It was the most heartfelt impulse of young men to go forth and do, but the sages held them to study. And as the young man grew older, full of energy and ambition, he could have wanted nothing less than to sit long hours in the discipline of the mind. To memorize and imitate, to argue and exposit, rather than to *do*—this was a stern test.

Nothing is so hard as to see one's contemporaries at their life's work and to postpone one's own. Nothing is so inviting as to pick up the burdens of the world and enter the workaday life, nor so demanding of self-discipline as to deny them. While others of his age were in the fields at home amassing their modest fortune in petty trade and acquiring the arts and crafts of the day, Yoḥanan and his fellow disciples sat at the feet of sages. They concentrated upon their learning, not with the curious but empty minds of infancy, but with all the strength of maturing, able men. But the conquest of the self— by overcoming ambition, distraction, and sheer laziness, by winning devotion to the mind, and by devoting the mind to Torah—these great struggles proved most satisfying of all when won. Later on no enemy proved so difficult as the enemy within. No battle could have proved harder to sustain than the one Yoḥanan fought in his own soul. Having vanquished his undisciplined impulse in the schoolhouse, he was ready for the struggle with the world. Having tasted the joy of learning, he never doubted the worth of the Torah's call to deeds. His later years, as we shall see, were years of renunciation. To Yoḥanan success was invariably denied. He rarely found testimony to the rightness of his viewpoint in the agreement of others. He walked apart. In the great crises of war and destruction he had finally to rely for strength only upon his own conviction. Torah had so filled the treasuries of heart and soul that it sustained a life of disappointment. It was at school that Yohanan was educated for life.

ii. Shammai and Hillel

"Rabban Yohanan ben Zakkai took over from Hillel and Shammai." He received from the earlier leaders of the Pharisees and transmitted to his disciples and thence to posterity a religious tradition concerning God, the world, and man. This tradition held that God had created the world. He cared for what happened in it. He had therefore told man his will. He demanded that man obey it. God had an ultimate purpose for human history which man might discern. Scripture was the vehicle for transmitting his will and plan. Together with ancient traditions about its meaning, revelation or "Torah" was the source of all instruction. Scriptural concerns extended to every aspect of the life of a "kingdom of priests and holy nation." Pharisaism also interested itself in affairs which today are regarded as secular. The Pharisees proposed policies to guide political, social, and economic affairs, as well as ritual activities. Viewed in their social setting, the Pharisees represented one among competing sects, for their coalition included only a small part of the nation. But their doctrines and breadth of interests applied to national and even universal questions.

Before the destruction of Jerusalem, however, the Pharisees administered only their own sectarian affairs. They did so through a central institution, a committee on which the leading sages held places. This council included the main factions among the Pharisees. At the turn of the first century, Hillel and Shammai stood at the head of the Pharisaic community. After the death of Hillel, his son Gamaliel I followed him. Simeon ben Gamaliel and Yohanan ben Zakkai succeeded approximately two decades before the rebellion of A.D. 66–70.

Shammai left relatively few sayings. On the whole, tradition did not grant him a "good press", for he was written up mainly by disciples of Hillel's followers. Thus Shammai was remembered for his petulance. He was presented as a foil to the implacably patient Hillel. We are told that Hillel was blessed by a convert: "May all the blessings of the Torah rest on your head! For had you been like Shammai the Elder, I might never have entered the community of Israel. The impatience of Shammai the Elder well nigh caused me to perish in this world and in the world to come. Your patience has brought me to the life of this world and of the world to come." While Yoḥanan was supposed to have succeeded Shammai as well as Hillel, he probably did not study with Shammai. Shammai left only three identifiable scriptural exegeses, which do not exhibit a characteristic method or viewpoint. The only common element one can discern between the teachings of Shammai and those of Yoḥanan is a superficial similarity of emphasis on cheerfulness and the study of Torah common to all the sages at this period. Thus Shammai said, "Fix a period for thy study of the Torah. Say little and do much, and receive all men with a cheerful countenance." Yoḥanan taught likewise.

Tradition explicitly claims that Hillel was Yoḥanan's teacher. Hillel had come from Baylonia about the last third of the first century B.C. He died in Jerusalem during the first quarter of the first century A.D. Hillel taught a methodology of interpreting Scripture which in time revolutionized the intellectual life of Pharisaism. These principles, known to exegetes of Greek classic texts as well, included the following: (1) Inference *a minori ad majus;* (2) inference by analogy; (3) constructing a family on the basis of one passage (extending a specific regulation of one biblical passage to a number of passages); (4) the same rule as the preceding, constructing a family on the basis of two biblical passages; (5) the general and the particular, the particular and the general; (6) exposition by means of another, similar passage; (7) deduction from the context. The Hillelite exegesis extended the potentialities of interpreting a given text in many ways. They thus made possible a very broad and liberal interpretation of Scripture. One can hardly overestimate the importance of Hillel's principles. Criticism today commonly uses the systematic principles of analogy, inference, association, and deduction. Before such principles became available, however, men were, as Professor Judah Goldin says,

> like primitive chemists deprived of catalytic agents. Phenomena surrounded them, but they suggested nothing new. Facts existed, but were incapable of reproducing anything surpassing themselves. Hillel recognized that tradition by itself was insufficient. . . . Its components had to be united . . . so that men would not be helpless when history was silent and they were left to their own resources.

Hillel is one of the truly enigmatic figures in Jewish history. We know some of his sayings, but little about what he did. His sayings reveal an irenic and humble man:

> Be of the disciples of Aaron, loving peace and pursuing it,
> Loving thy fellow-creatures.
> And drawing them near to the Torah.
> A name made great is a name destroyed.

At the same time, he stressed the importance of learning:

> He who does not increase his knowledge diminishes it.
> He who does not study deserves to die.
> He who makes profane use of the crown of Torah will waste away.

His most famous saying is:

> If I am not for myself, who will be for me?
> But when I am for myself alone, what am I?
> And if not now, when?

He fervently believed in Providence; seeing a skull floating in a stream, he said,

> Because you drowned others, you have been drowned.
> But they who drowned you will themselves be drowned.

His view of worldly possessions was skeptically realistic:

> The more flesh, the more worms; the more property, the more anxiety; the more women, the more witchcraft . . . . But the more Torah, the more life; the more schooling, the more wisdom; the more counsel, the more understanding; the more charity, the more peace. He who has acquired a good name has acquired it for himself, but he who has acquired for himself words of Torah has acquired for himself life in the world to come.

Stress upon study of the Torah as the key to eternal life suggests that for Hillel study meant more than the acquisition of worldly information. It included insight into the principles underlying all reality. Torah contained the secrets of the universe. It was, therefore, the instrument by which men would achieve truth about God who made the world and gave the Torah. Worldly possessions meant little, not because asceticism was of value in its own right, but because wealth impeded man's search for truth by imposing worries and concerns. His stress upon Providence suggests a strong belief in the need for faith itself. Men may be perfectly certain of receiving their just reward. Hence they should not join those of little faith who worry about worldly necessities. Love for humanity, study of Torah, service to Creator and creature alike—these are the central emphases of Hillel's sayings. As we shall see, at Yavneh Yoḥanan ben Zakkai did little more than recover and renew his master's words and present them as the guiding principles of the new age.

As head of the Pharisees Hillel promulgated a series of emergency ordinances (*taqqanot*) to meet the crises of his time. The device of issuing such decrees was also employed by Gamaliel I and Yoḥanan. One decree was aimed at circumventing the effect of the law of sabbatical year on outstanding loans. This law (Deut. 15:2) had commanded that in the seventh year of the septennial cycle all outstanding loans and other debts were automatically annulled. Originally a protection for the debtor, the law intended to prevent his becoming burdened with an endlessly multiplying debt by limiting the tenure of financial obligation. Its effect by the time of Hillel had been to diminish the availability of loans in the final years of the cycle. The poor, therefore, could not obtain the loans absolutely necessary for subsistence in the seasonal agricultural economy. Hillel enacted a legal instrument called *prozbul,* by which the lender gave into the hands of a court the record of all his loans. To the court the biblical injunction did not apply. The loans were then not annulled by the seventh year. A second such ordinance dealt with the biblical decree that houses sold in ancient cities might be reclaimed by their original owners within a year of the sale by restoring the purchase price. The new owners resorted to a ruse, hiding out during the end of the period of grace so that the seller could not return their money. Hillel decreed that the court might act in behalf of the original owner even in the absence of the purchaser. He thus showed himself keenly aware of the interplay between law and social order.

If, as tradition alleged, Yoḥanan studied with Hillel, one understands certain qualities which characterized both men. It would have been from Hillel that Yoḥanan acquired his dedication to the ideal of peace, for Hillel had said, "Be of the disciples of Aaron, loving peace, pursuing peace, loving mankind, and drawing all men to Torah." From Hillel Yoḥanan would have learned that the sage has the responsibility to concern himself with pressing social problems. Hillel, moreover, had laid the foundation for his public career through many decades of study, and Yoḥanan did likewise. He also would have learned the usefulness of the special decree to deal with a crisis. He decreed changes in law which were far more substantial than the social ordinances of Hillel. He struck out provisions of the Temple cult which men believed were of Mosaic origin. He took into account by further enactments the profound transformation of the liturgical life after the destruction of the Temple. Hillel had taught, "One who does not study deserves to die." Yoḥanan said that man was created in order to study the Torah. Hillel had admonished, "Do not trust yourself until the day you die." Both Yoḥanan and his student Eliezer ben Hyrcanus developed this idea in their parables. Of both Hillel and Yoḥanan fabulous feats of learning were reported. To both a life span of one hundred twenty years was ascribed. Finally, Hillel's teaching "In a place where is no man, strive to be a man" epitomized Yoḥanan's conduct during the revolution and afterward.

What kind of teacher could Hillel have been? One must suppose that he preferred patience and gentleness to rigorous dispute. Keeping the students' attention focused upon the real issues, Hillel would have spoken in deceptively simple terms. What indeed could be simpler than the phrase, "If I am not for myself, who will be for me?" No student could have missed the point. A man is responsible for his own welfare. The next sentence may have troubled the student, "But if I am only for myself, then what am I?" Here, too, the student must have understood his teacher's message to mean, "One should not be selfish." But the two sentences were followed by a third, "If not now, when?" What indeed is the master asking? Is there some veiled mystery underneath these plain words? The student would have had to ponder many days to come to an understanding of these simple sentences.

Similarly, Hillel taught a rule which would have taken his students many years to spell out: "What is hateful to yourself, do not to your fellow. That is the whole Torah. All the rest is commentary. Now go forth and learn!" Such a rule, based upon the passage every Jew knew by heart, "Thou shalt love thy neighbor as thyself" (Lev. 19:18), could not have represented anything new. And yet when the student heard, "That is the whole Torah," he must have been troubled. He knew many other, equally important passages in the Torah, beginning with the Ten Commandments, or "In the beginning, God created the heaven and the earth," or "Righteousness, righteousness pursue." The student's perplexity must have been deepened when he heard the words, "All the rest is commentary." Was Hillel telling him that all the other teachings of the Torah *must* be related to the ethical principle, and that theology, law, and ritual were really subsumed under the principle of love of neighbor? What of love for God? Love for self, which Hillel also recommended? And then the master said, "Now go forth and learn." The student must have wondered, Where is he to go to learn if not to the academy? Was Hillel telling him that here, where student and master met together, learning did not take place? So the master spoke and the disciple listened; the one speaking both to his day and to the ages, the other privileged to hear for the first time words which have echoed through the centuries. The student heard and wondered what the master meant and began the task of finding out. He was the first, but the last has not yet come, to ponder the words of Hillel.

iii. Hillel's Disciple

Hillel had eighty disciples. The eldest was Jonathan ben 'Uzziel, and the youngest, Yohanan ben Zakkai. Jonathan mastered mystical lore. It was reported that when he would sit and study Torah, birds flying overhead would be burned up. He also translated the prophetic books of the Bible into Aramaic:

> A heavenly voice was heard to proclaim, "Who is this that reveals the Lord's secret to man?"
> Jonathan answered, "It is I who have revealed God's secrets to man, but I have not done this for my own honor, nor for that of my father's house, but for the honor of God, that dissension may not increase in Israel."
> He intended to translate the Writings as well, but another voice went forth and shouted, "Enough!"

Since these "secrets" were not published, we may only speculate about what they concerned. They must have involved a theosophical understanding of Scriptures. Simple stories were given metaphysical significations and prophetic visions of God, such as those of Isaiah and Ezekiel, were spelled out in some detail. As we shall see, the mystical tradition of Hillel and Jonathan ben 'Uzziel was maintained by Yohanan.

Hillel and Shammai gave their names to two schools of thought within Pharisaism, the School of Hillel and the School of Shammai. Three hundred and sixteen controversies between the two schools were recorded with the Shammaites on "the strict side" in all but fifty-five of them. The debates had to do mostly with ritual and legal matters. But one of the debates dealt with a more fundamental question: Was it good that man had been created? Might it have been better if he had been left uncreated? The schools spent two and one-half years on the question. The Hillelites argued the affirmative, the Shammaites the negative. They finally agreed that it would have been better if man had not been created, but since he had been created, he ought to reflect upon his actions. Of the students of Shammai, only three are known by name: Bava ben Butah, Dositai of Kfar Yarma, and Ẓaddoq. The second is mentioned only once, and the third supposedly ruled invariably according to the Hillelite opinion. Bava ben Butah was remembered for his extraordinary piety. He was said to have brought a sin offering to the Temple every day of the year, except for the Day of Atonement, to atone for any guilt he might unknowingly have incurred.

The absolute *terminus ad quem* of Hillel's life appears to be in the twenties of the first century, when his son began to preside over the Pharisaic academy. This much becomes clear from the evidence of the apostle Paul, who stated, "I am a Jew, born at Tarsus . . . but brought up in this city [Jerusalem] at the feet of Gamaliel." (Acts 22:3, 26:4; Gal. 1:14). If Saul was born about A.D. 10 and went up to Jerusalem as a youth, perhaps about A.D., 25 then Gamaliel must have presided by the middle of the fourth decade of the first century. He was certainly a respected teacher of the law and a member of the Sanhedrin by the year A.D., 35 for when Jesus' followers were persecuted by the priests and Sadducees, they were defended by him (Acts 5:33). If Hillel had been in the Sanhedrin, these traditions would not likely have hidden that fact. There is no evidence, on the other hand, to suggest that Hillel died two decades earlier, except the tradition that he had a son Simeon; but even if such a son had lived and succeeded his father, he made absolutely no mark whatever on the traditional consciousness, and it may be supposed that he held office for a very short time. Hillel might have lived, therefore, to A.D. 20-25. If Yoḥanan had entered the academy as a youth, he might well have been the youngest of Hillel's students. It is known that students were received at a very early age. One therefore cannot say that Yoḥanan certainly did not study with Hillel. It is at least possible that he did. If so, however, his studies with Hillel could not have lasted for a very long time. We must recognize that the desire to claim continuity of Pharisaic leadership, from Hillel before the destruction to Yoḥanan ben Zakkai after it, motivated the ascription of such discipleship.

Another tradition, however, holds that Yoḥanan came to Hillel's school in his mature years:

> *And Moses was one hundred twenty years old* (Deut. 34:7). He was one of four who died at one hundred twenty: Moses, and Hillel the Elder, and Rabban Yoḥanan ben Zakkai, and Rabbi 'Aqiva.
>
> Moses was in Egypt forty years, in Midian forty years, and sustained Israel forty years.
>
> Hillel the Elder went up from Babylonia aged forty years, served as apprentice to the sages forty years, and sustained Israel forty years.
>
> Rabban Yoḥanan ben Zakkai occupied himself in commerce forty years, served as apprentice to the sages forty years, and forty years he sustained Israel.
>
> Rabbi 'Aqiva was a shepherd forty years, studied Torah forty years, and sustained Israel forty years.
>
> There were six pairs whose life span was identical: Rebecca and Kahath, Levi and Amram, Joseph and Joshua, Samuel and Solomon, Moses and Hillel the Elder, Rabban Yoḥanan ben Zakkai and Rabbi 'Aqiva.

Hillel had eighty disciples of whom it was recorded:

> Thirty of them were worthy to have the Presence of God rest upon them as upon Moses our master, but their generation was unworthy of it. Thirty of them were worthy to determine and calculate the calendar, and twenty of them were middling. The eldest of them was Jonathan ben 'Uzziel. The least of them all was Rabban Yoḥanan ben Zakkai.

As Hillel lay dying, his students gathered at his bedside to take leave of him. But Yoḥanan did not enter with them:

> Hillel asked, "And where is Yoḥanan?"
> "There he is, standing outside the door," the students answered.
> "Let him enter, he is worthy," Hillel said.
> When he had entered, Hillel said to the students, "The youngest of you is father of wisdom and father of the future—and the oldest among you, how much the more so!"
> He added, "And concerning all of you Scripture speaks, *I [Wisdom] walk in the way of righteousness, in the path of justice, endowing with wealth those who love me, and filling their treasuries*" (Prov. 8:21-36).
> "And concerning you, Yoḥanan, Scripture says the same, *. . . endowing with wealth.*"

Thus posterity envisioned how the master's cloak was laid upon the shoulders of the young Yoḥanan. Yoḥanan probably remained a student for a considerable time after Hillel's death. He was one of those legendary students who leave behind incredible stories about their scholarship and diligence. Thus it was told of Yoḥanan ben Zakkai:

> He did not neglect a single Scripture or Mishnah, *Gemara* [explanation of Mishnah], *halakhah* [law], *aggada* [legend], supplement [branch of the oral law] or the subtleties of Scripture, or the subtleties of the scribes, or any of the sages' rules of interpretation—not a single thing in the Torah did he neglect, confirming the statement, *That I may cause those that love me to inherit substance, and that I may fill their treasuries.*

It was also said of him that he never in his life engaged in idle conversation:

> He never went four cubits without words of Torah and without *tefillin*, either winter or summer. None ever preceded him into the schoolhouse. He never fell asleep in the schoolhouse, either accidentally or intentionally. He never left anyone in the schoolhouse. None ever found him sleeping there. None ever opened the door to his students but himself. He never made a

statement which he had not first heard from his master. He never said, "The hour has come to arise from our studies," except on the afternoon before Passover and before the Day of Atonement, and so did Rabbi Eliezer his student after him.

Yoḥanan said: "If all the heavens were parchment, and all the trees pens, and all the oceans ink, they would not suffice to write down the wisdom which I have learned from my masters, and I took away from them no more than a fly takes from the sea when it bathes." So too his student Eliezer ben Hyrcanus said: "If all the seas were ink, and all the reeds pens, and all men scribes, they could not write down all the Scripture and Mishnah I studied, not what I learned from the sages in the academy. Yet I carried away from my teachers no more than does a man who dips his finger in the sea, and I gave away to my disciples no more than a paintbrush takes from the tube."

iv. *"O Galilee, Galilee!"*

Sometime after the death of Hillel, Yoḥanan left Jerusalem for Galilee where he settled in a village called 'Arav, bringing with him his wife and young son. No source states explicitly when Yoḥanan went to Galilee, though it is quite certain that he was there.

We have several indications that the Galilee period came relatively early in his life. First, he was married and had a young son at that time. If, as was common, he married about the age of twenty, then his son's relative youth would imply that he was in Galilee sometime between A.D. 20 and A.D. 40. Second, he was not well known at this time, for only two cases were brought to him during the entire period of his Galilee sojourn. Third Ḥanina ben Dosa, his student in 'Arav, came to him in Galilee to begin his study of Torah. Since Ḥanina lived well before the destruction of Jerusalem, he may have come at an early age. Yoḥanan probably did not teach him during his Jerusalem period, for Ḥanina is omitted from all lists of the Jerusalem circle. Fourth, as we shall see, Yoḥanan returned to Jerusalem while Gamaliel I was still president of the Pharisees. Since the Jerusalem period continued uninterruptedly until the destruction, one must date the Galilee period either before A.D. 45 or after A.D. 70. The period after the destruction was spent entirely at Yavneh and Beror Ḥayil. Furthermore, after the destruction, he was an old man and unlikely to have had a young son.

We do not know why Yoḥanan went to Galilee. The region was not, as I said, a center of "study of Torah" in the manner and traditions of the Pharisees. Yoḥanan entered some kind of business. We do not know exactly what he did, merely that he was in trade. All the rabbis of this time supported themselves through business, farming, crafts, or as common laborers. The rabbinate was not a paid profession, but a lifelong calling. The rabbi may have exerted great influence, but that did not result in much economic benefit. It was forbidden to "use the Torah as a spade to dig with." Teaching was not compensated, nor was presiding in court. Each rabbi provided for himself as best he could. A few were well-to-do, but most were not. Those who were rich were unable to support many others, though they did maintain students. In later times rabbis presided over the fortunes of whole Jewish communities, even while they made a living in the humblest occupations. No one thought it strange or associated wealth with wisdom. It was not riches which authenticated the teachings of a sage. A poor man was not disqualified by his poverty. Indeed, none discerned an intrinsic relationship between worldly resources and communal status. It was not the position that one held which made a difference, but what he knew and could accomplish. It was later taught that the title does not honor the man, but the man the title.

Having gone into trade, Yoḥanan settled in 'Arav. One wonders why he could not have done equally well in Jerusalem or in one of the villages in the coastal plain. We have no evidence that Yoḥanan was sent to 'Arav as an apostle of the Pharisaic movement. On the other hand, he did decide a number of legal cases and taught. It stands to reason that the Pharisaic group thought it necessary to station some of its leading members in various parts of the country to make certain its legal and moral principles were everywhere available. But the Galileans, relatively recently converted to Judaism, could not have been deeply interested in strictly legal questions. Their chief concern, as depicted in the Synoptic Gospels, was for miraculous salvation. "What must I do to be saved?"

What was it that they wished to be saved *from*? According to the Gospel accounts they wanted to be healed of sickness, cured of blindness and lameness, and rid of the demons that afflicted their souls. It was therefore a private, trivial, this-worldly salvation which the people wanted. Unless initiated into the Pharisaic view of Torah, they could not have understood the connection between the "Torah" of a sage such as Yoḥanan and their immediate concerns. We have no similar accounts of Jerusalemites, but if we had, one would hardly be surprised to find the same stress upon the workaday matters of healing and exorcism which today are the preserve of medicine and psychiatry. What did the Galileans wish to be saved *for*? The answer is equally clear. They wanted eternal life or life in the world to come. The "kingdom of heaven" meant this much at least. Men would not finally die, but live under God's dominion. This accounts for the fiery enthusiasm of the Zealots and other "brigands" who endlessly came out of the hills to plague Roman administrators. In bringing the Messiah, they would ensure as well their own salvation. Ideas concerning personal salvation, eschatological fulfillment, the life of the world to come, the heavenly Eden, and the like fused in an explosive mixture. Energies released in their combination in time would devastate the land.

What did Yoḥanan have to offer the Galileans? He taught a more difficult way to salvation. His way demanded the boldness to believe that learning—"Torah"—would bear cosmic consequences. To what did such learning pertain? Humble matters of daily life, which no one could believe would really affect tomorrow, let alone the final climax and end of all time, were the objects of his teaching. Yoḥanan was not a healer, nor did he preach a quick or facile conclusion of history. He did not call men to an easy commitment. He did not promise the world to come, though that was implicit in his doctrines, but rather ultimate seriousness about *this* life. Where men wanted to hear that they could do something of historical, even other-worldly consequence, he turned their attention to the inconsequential matter of how they behaved toward the neighbor whom they saw every day. From those who wanted to bear witness to their courage on the battlefield he called for brave but quiet actions in the home, field, and marketplace. Some would readily give up all in a splendid moment of self-abnegation. Yohanan told them, in the words of his teacher, that they remained responsible for themselves, but not for themselves alone, and the time is now. The doctrines he brought from Jerusalem, the tasks he may have been assigned to carry out, the goals he set for himself: nothing could have been less appropriate to the spiritual condition of Galilee.

Ascending from the coastal plain to the foothills of the lower Galilee, Yohanan first spied the town of 'Arav, near Sepphoris. There he was to live for eighteen years. He settled down with his wife and young son to teach Torah. The town, containing a large number of priestly families, was listed among those providing a "watch" in the Temple service, that is, priests to do the Temple duties for a time, as representative of the whole. There Yohanan acted as teacher and magistrate. Two cases of Sabbath law were brought to him, and he judged both severely, though with hesitation. The first was this: On the Sabbath may one cover a scorpion with a dish so that it will not sting anyone? Is this considered an act of hunting (destruction of life), which therefore would be forbidden on the Sabbath? When the case was brought to Yohanan, he stated: "I doubt whether he is not liable to bring a sin-offering for such an act." The decision in the second case was reported in exactly the same words. The record of both was preserved in a single document, later incorporated into the Mishnah.

In the third century, 'Ulla, an Amora in Palestine, stated: "Eighteen years Rabban Yohanan ben Zakkai spent in 'Arav, and only these two cases came before him. At the end he said, 'O Galilee, Galilee! You hate the Torah! Your end will be to be besieged!' " Yoḥanan had only one student in Galilee, Ḥanina ben Dosa. Ḥanina remained behind after Yoḥanan returned to Jerusalem. He was renowned for his piety, and celebrated as a faith healer and intercessor:

> When the son of Gamaliel was ill, he sent two disciples to Ḥanina to ask his prayers in the boy's behalf. When Ḥanina saw them, he went to the upper chamber of his house and prayed for mercy. When he came down, he said to the disciples, "Go, for his fever has left him."
>
> "And are you a prophet?" they asked.
>
> "I am neither a prophet nor the disciple of a prophet, but if prayer is fluent in my mouth, I know that it is accepted, and if not, I know that it is rejected."
>
> The disciples sat down and wrote a letter, fixing the very hour of the day [so as to know whether a true miracle had taken place].
>
> When they returned to Jerusalem, Gamaliel said to them, "By the Temple service! You neither subtracted nor added, but it happened at that exact moment his fever broke and he asked us for water to drink."

Ḥanina was likewise an ascetic, and one day an echo came for and was heard to say:

> All the world is fed on account of Ḥanina my son, and Ḥanina my son subsists on a basket of carobs from week to week.

His teaching in the chain of tradition was:

> He in whom the spirit of his fellow man takes delight, in him the spirit of the Omnipresent takes delight, and he in whom the spirit of his fellow creatures takes no delight, in him the spirit of the Omnipresent takes no delight.

Likewise he taught:

> "He whose fear of sin takes precedence over his wisdom, his wisdom shall endure, as it is said, *We shall do and we shall harken*" (Exod. 24:7). He whose wisdom takes precedence

over his fear of sin, his wisdom shall not endure, as it is said, *The fear of the Lord is the beginning of wisdom"* (Ps. 111:10).

He used to say, "He whose works exceeds his wisdom, his wisdom shall endure, as it is said, *We shall do and we shall harken"* (Exod. 24:7).

These teachings may well have been influenced by Yoḥanan, who taught:

> If one is wise and fears sin, what is he like? Lo, he is a crafts-man with the tools of his craft in his hand. If one is wise and does not fear sin, what is he like? Lo, he is a craftsman without the tools of his craft in his hand. If one fears sin but is not wise, what is he like? He is not a craftsman, but the tools of his craft are in his hand.

One discerns a difference in the attitude of a disciple, for while Ḥanina said nothing about one who is fearful of sin but not learned, Yoḥanan specifically criticized such a man. Like Hillel, Yoḥanan emphasized that knowledge of the Torah was the prerequisite of piety. The difference in viewpoints came out in their first encounter. When Ḥanina ben Dosa came to study with Yoḥanan ben Zakkai in 'Arav, it happened that Yoḥanan's son was deathly sick. He said to him:

> "Ḥanina, my son, seek mercy for him that he may live."
> Ḥanina put his head between his knees, and prayed for mercy, and the boy lived.
> Rabban Yoḥanan ben Zakkai said to him, "If Ben Zakkai were to throw his head down between his knees all day long, none would pay attention to him."
> Yoḥanan's wife then said to him, "And is Ḥanina greater than you?"
> "No," he replied, "but he is like a slave before the King, and I am like a prince before the King."

What did this comparison mean? Yoḥanan was comparing the relationship between Ḥanina and God to that of a slave and a king, and his own to that of a prince and a king. During this very period the control of the Roman government was passing from the hands of elected public officials of the Senatorial class ("princes before the king") to favorites, even to slaves of the imperial household. In later years under Nero the lives of great public officials were not safe. Any slight offense might lead to their execution under the capricious monarch. But favorite slaves of the emperor had a free hand. Yoḥanan seemed to make a complaint. Such is the way of God. He has favorite slaves, such as Ḥanina, who get their way by importuning. But the great ministers of state, such as the masters of Torah, are compelled to uphold the most rigorous standards. His statement is consistent with the sages' earlier criticism of Honi the Circler, in the time of Simeon b. Shetaḥ (ca. 80 B.C.), an earlier miracle worker and rainmaker: "If it were not that you are Honi, I would have pronounced a ban of excommunication against you! But what shall I do to you! You importune God and he performs your will, like a son that importunes his father and he performs his will. Of you Scripture says, 'Let your father and your mother be glad, and let her that bore you rejoice'" (Prov. 23:25). Yoḥanan thus gave expression to the tension he felt between himself and the Galilean environment. Pharisaic sages were few. Fewer still were those who consulted them. He found in Galilee that none came to seek his learning, and left behind him a bitter curse, "O Galilee Galilee! You hate the Torah!"

v. Zaccheus/Zakkai

The apocryphal Gospel of Thomas preserves stories about Jesus' encounter with a Galilean schoolteacher by the name of Zaccheus. Having heard Jesus' wonderful sayings, Zaccheus offered to teach the child letters, all knowledge, and good manners (presumably Torah and *derekh'erez*). When, however, Zaccheus taught the child the first letter, Jesus replied:

> "Thou who art ignorant of the nature of the Alpha, how can you teach others the Beta?" . . . Then he began to question the teacher about the first letter, and he was not able to answer him. When the teacher Zaccheus heard the child speaking such-

and-so great allegories of the first letter, he was at a great loss
. . . about his teaching, and he said to those that were present,
"Alas, I, wretch that I am, am at a loss, bringing shame upon
myself by having dragged this child hither. . . . I cannot get at
his meaning: thrice wretched that I am, I have deceived myself.
I tried to have a student, and was found to have a teacher. My
mind is filled with shame . . . because I, an old man, have been
conquered by a child."

The apocryphal gospel contains a relatively ancient tradition,
for a variant of the story without the name Zaccheus is referred
to by Irenaeus. By the end of the second century, a heterodox
tradition, probably gnostic, preserved the story, and the tradition, was known and had to be refuted as far to the west as
Lyons.

One is struck by the fact that the name Zaccheus is known
to have been borne by a Galilean contemporary of Jesus.
Yoḥanan was known as "ben Zakkai," and that Zaccheus would
represent the Greek translation for "ben Zakkai" is hardly im-
plausible. Jesus vanquished a teacher of the law by the name
of Zaccheus, and Yoḥanan ben Zakkai was a Galilean teacher
for part of his life. Can one offer a plausible explanation for
the apocryphal story?

No one has argued that the apocryphal gospels contain
precise historical data. We cannot hope to find in them reliable information about either Yoḥanan or Jesus. But the
legend itself is a fact requiring explanation. In what *situation*
would a story about Jesus and "Zaccheus" have been particularly relevant? I suggest that the story arose, in its original
form, in the Jewish Christian community in Galilee after
A.D. 70, and that it was intended to liberate the community
from the authority of Yoḥanan's academy at Yavneh. Among
the Jewish-Christians, the name of Rabban Yoḥanan ben Zakkai must have been well known after A.D. 70, for he founded
at Yavneh a central institution which promulgated laws applying to Palestinian Judaism. In so doing, he advanced the
claim that the continuity of Jewish religious and legal institutions had *not* ceased with the destruction of Jerusalem, nor

had God rejected Israel; indeed, some of his decrees suggest that he had assumed the prerogatives of the Temple administration. Those who held that the destruction of Jerusalem represented divine retribution for the rejection and crucifixion of Jesus could hardly acknowledge the continuity of Jewish religious authority or the legitimacy of Yoḥanan's institution at Yavneh.

If the Jerusalem community, now in refuge at Pella, was unaware of the importance of the claim advanced at Yavneh, those Jewish-Christians in heavily Jewish districts such as in Galilee must have known about it. They doubtless gave thought, therefore, to the issue of whether Yavneh had truly inherited the charisma and authority of the Jerusalem Temple. Denying the legitimacy of that inheritance would have been substantially easier if Yoḥanan himself had been preplexed and confounded by Jesus, even forced to admit that "he surpasseth me, I shall not attain to his understanding." This would have settled the issue once for all, even among those Jewish-Christians who were disposed to remain under the law. We cannot say who told the story, but we may conclude that it was important to tell it in Galilee after the year 70. The germ of the story was that Zakkai/Zaccheus had been vanquished at his own métier by the child Jesus. Since Zaccheus laid such great emphasis on the study of the Torah, claiming that his academy's superior traditions warranted its activities, Zaccheus' acknowledgment of the superior learning of Jesus rendered inconsequential any claim he might now press for authority over the Jewish-Christians. They might have accepted the decisions of the Temple authorities. They would never accept those of a teacher of the law discredited by the child Jesus. The content of the story need not have remained constant; indeed, for translation into Greek it could not. It was drastically reshaped from the time it was first told, and the detail of Zaccheus' name was retained long after it ceased to be relevant.

We do not know, as I said, whether this is a true story. Since for a time they lived within a few miles of one another, it is possible that the two did meet. But if they had, I doubt

that they would have realized how very far apart their followers would diverge. Yoḥanan accepted Ḥanina as a student
and taught him, so he did not think ill of miracle-workers.
Like others, he believed in their powers. Jesus for his part
preached an ethical message which laid stress on loving one's
neighbor and similar cherished beliefs of Hillel in particular
and of Pharisaic Judaism in general. If the Gospel accounts
provide an accurate record, Jesus' message, apart from his
alleged claim to personally usher in the kingdom of God,
would have won considerable respect from Yoḥanan.

vi. Conclusion

The Pharisaic sages sought to administer the inner life of
Israel in accordance with their understanding of the ancient
body of legal and prophetic literature. This prophecy could
not be contradicted later on, for God would not change his
mind. He did not need to repeat himself. He did not have
to rehearse the authenticating acts which had originally vin-
dicated his word. The sages, therefore, did not advance a
claim to unconditional prophetic authority, as did their contemporary, Jesus of Nazareth, or to miraculous abilities, as
did Ḥanina ben Dosa. The sages, and Yoḥanan among them,
followed a middle way between the spontaneous religion of
Galilee which looked for daily miracles, signs, and wonders,
and the loyal literalism of the Jerusalem priesthood which
held fast to Scripture's commandments concerning the sacri-
cial cult. In Galilee Yoḥanan encountered the opposite of the
rigid traditional routine of the priests. His student possessed
wonderful healing gifts. Yoḥanan contrasted Ḥanina's power
with his own. He found himself in a region in which the
ancient faith of Israel was still new and fluid. Men there
eagerly asked one another as well as itinerant preachers what
they must do to keep the faith, because they could not look
back upon forefathers who for many generations had done
things thus and so. Though they kept "Judaism" with the
zealous eagerness of converts and the children of converts,
what it really consisted of and demanded was by no means

finally established. Theirs was an open, primitive, unlettered faith, pure and all-embracing, but with more enthusiasm than discipline. Most of all it was a faith for the hour and the day, not handed down from olden times, but tested moment by moment.

Yoḥanan could not share that kind of piety. In Jerusalem, however, he found that the vision of his early years, the memories of a sacred routine set down at Sinai and carried on with perfect loyalty ever since, would prove no more than an illusion. He remembered Jerusalem for its serenity. It was his own happiness that he recalled. He thought of the beauty and sanctity of the Temple. It was the pure and innocent recollection of youth that had adorned the worldly sanctuary with heavenly splendor. When he first came to Jerusalem, young and not yet disappointed in life, he saw all things through the spectacles of hope. He turned back in uncertain middle age, more a failure than a success. Jerusalem would also have to undergo the examination of a mature, more discerning consciousness.

He said Galilee hated the Torah. But would he find that Jerusalem loved it? He was not consulted in Galilee. Would he now be besieged with inquiries by the men of Jerusalem? He rejected the piety of Galilee, for it was unformed and too fresh. But would the mellow but fatigued piety of Jerusalem better conform to his conception? He turned his back upon the north, and once more ascended the foothills. Climbing up to the holy city, he shared the company of tradesmen, soldiers, and pilgrims speaking strange tongues and wearing outlandish clothes. Most were Jews to be sure, but so different from one another that he must have wondered what made these various men into one "Israel."

He must have thought back, now in the middle years of life, to the happy day when his father first took him up to the Temple, and again to the exciting moment when he first came by himself. Once, Jerusalem had been new to him. Now what would he find there? The city of his memory and with it the refreshing hope of the young man? Or would Jerusalem disappoint him as had Galilee?

He was growing old, yet remained of no importance. His wife was jealous of his honor and with reason enough. Now must come the time to keep the well-meant promises of youth. Here he had to do the great deeds he once had dreamed of doing for the sake of Torah. If not now, when? If not here, where? Not on some distant tomorrow when he would be too old. Not in Galilee, where he had failed. But surely here, in the center of learning and sanctity. Surely now, at the height of his powers. He reached the gate, and then his feet were within the walls of Jerusalem. For a moment he must have felt mingled awe and fear, awe for the city, fear for his own strength to do the task he had long before set for himself.

III. Mighty Hammer

i. Return to Jerusalem

Yoḥanan ben Zakkai returned to Jerusalem a disappointed man. Nearing forty, he had little to show for his labors but a mixed record at best: one student—and he was a miracle worker—two cases of peripheral interest, an ailing son, and a bitter wife. A life of Torah was not supposed to produce worldly benefit, but to Yoḥanan it had not brought anything else either. What had Hillel's most distinguished student accomplished after the years of study and apprenticeship? Ahead lay further decades of thwarted hopes. Jerusalem in the mid-first century showed no greater interest in Torah than had Galilee.

While it is not entirely certain when Yoḥanan returned to Jerusalem, one may conjecture that he arrived during the tenure of Gamaliel I as president of the Pharisaic party, about the year A.D. 40. First, he was active in Jerusalem for a considerable period before the Revolution of 66, for by 62, it was alleged, he represented the Pharisees in certain disputes with the Sadducees. Even earlier, however, he was associated with Simeon ben Gamaliel in the leadership of the Pharisaic group. If, as is commonly assumed, Simeon assumed office about the year 50 and if Yoḥanan's authority was coterminus with Simeon's, then one must conjecture that Yoḥanan had lived in the city for at least some years to achieve leadership in the Pharisaic community. Second, he certainly exerted some authority during Gamaliel's presidency, since one of his teachings was effectively vitiated by a special enactment of Gamaliel. Third, Yoḥanan's student Joshua ben Hananiah was born about 30–

35. If he came to Yoḥanan's academy at the usual age, that is, about thirteen or fourteen, then Yoḥanan must certainly have been teaching in Jerusalem by the end of the fifth decade of the first century. Hence, it seems not unlikely that Yoḥanan returned to Jerusalem during the tenure of Gamaliel I and probably well before his death which allegedly took place about 50. This would suggest that Yoḥanan had arrived about the year 40.

ii. The Priests and the Pharisees

In Jerusalem Yoḥanan encountered a kind of religion quite different in emphasis from that of his Galilean student Ḥanina ben Dosa. It was a cultic religion administered by the priests of the Temple. Like other peoples in ancient times Jews believed that all kinds of sacrifices, public and private, propitiated God and achieved forgiveness for sin. There was indeed sufficient foundation for such a belief. Scripture had ordained various animal offerings for many spiritual purposes. The priesthood, as loyal to Scripture as the Pharisaic sages, was internationally famous for its disciplined devotion to the Temple and for the exactness and solemnity with which the Temple service was carried on. The priests were remembered by the Pharisees, their critics:

> It says, *Open your doors, O Lebanon, that the fire may consume thy cedars* (Zech. 11:1). This refers to the high priests who were in the Temple.
> They took their keys in their hands and threw them up to the sky, saying to the Holy One, blessed be He, "Master of the Universe, here are the keys which thou didst hand over to us, for we have not been trustworthy custodians to do the king's work and to eat of the king's table."

Despite this polemic, the Pharisees recognized the legitimacy of the cult, participated in its ceremonies, mourned at its cessation, and longed for its restoration. After the destruction, Joshua ben Ḥananiah would exclaim, "Woe unto us, that this, the place here the iniquities of Israel were atoned for, is laid waste." Likewise, the termination of the Temple service was considered by Pharisaic doctrine to be a disaster for the world: "So long as the Temple service is maintained, the world is a blessing to its inhabitants and the rains come in season . . . but when the Temple service is not maintained, the world is not a blessing to its inhabitants and rains do not come in season."

The sages, following some of the prophets, thus accepted the legitimacy of the sacrificial service, teaching, like the prophets, that true repentance must accompany sin and guilt offerings: "If a man said, I will sin and repent, and sin and again repent, he will be given no chance to repent." The sages found much to criticize, however, in the character of the priesthood. The high priests, depending on political connections with Rome for their appointment, certainly did not heed Pharisaic instructions. The Pharisees claimed to possess the true interpretation of Scripture concerning even cultic practices. Priestly indifference to their pretensions became a source of considerable irritation. Some priests were moreover reputed in Pharisaic traditions and elsewhere to be arrogant and heavy-handed in claiming their sacerdotal benefits. Thus Josephus reported:

Hananiah likewise had servants who were very wicked. They joined themselves to the boldest sort of the people, and went to the threshing floors and took away by violence the tithes that belonged to the priests. They did not refrain from beating those who would not give these tithes to them. So the other high priests acted in like manner, as did his servants. No one was able to stop them, so that some of the priests who were accustomed to being supported from those tithes died for want of food.

A popular song, preserved in Pharisaic literature, went:

Woe unto me because of the house of Boethus
Woe unto me because of their clubs!
Woe unto me because of the house of Ḥanin
Woe unto me because of their whisperings!

Woe unto me because of the house of Kathros,
Woe unto me because of their quills.
Woe unto me because of the house of Ishmael ben Phiabi,
Woe unto me because of their fists.
For they are high priests,
And their sons are treasurers.
And their sons-in-law are law-officers,
And their slaves beat the folk with sticks.

The Pharisaic teacher, Rabbi Ẓaddoq, rebuked the priests for their violence. It once happened that two priests, equal in rank, were running up the Temple ramp to the altar. One got up the ramp before the other. The one behind took a knife and stabbed the first through the heart:

> Rabbi, Ẓaddoq stood up on the stairs of the Great Hall and said, "Oh our brothers, children of Israel, hear! Behold it is written, *If in the land which the Lord your God gives you to possess, anyone is found slain, lying in the open country, and it is not known who killed him, then your elders and your judges shall come forth, and they shall measure the distance to the cities which are around the corpse, and the elders of the city which is nearest to the slain man shall take a heifer . . . and all of the elders of that city nearest to the slain man shall wash their hands over the heifer whose neck was broken in the valley, and they shall testify that our hands did not shed this blood. . . . Forgive, O Lord, Your people Israel whom You have redeemed, and set not the guilt of innocent blood in the midst of Your people Israel.* (Deut. 21:1-9). We—for whom shall we bring the heifer? For the city? Or for the Temple court?"

Reports of cultic corruption, however, ought to be treated with considerable caution. Many of the priests and Sadducees were patriots. They stood in the forefront of the later revolutionary movement. Others counted themselves among the Pharisaic party. Pharisaic literature itself attests to the loyalty to scriptural precepts which characterized the administration of the Temple. To think of the leading Sadducees as generally ignorant or corrupt is to be misled by Pharisaic propaganda.

The rabbis preserved their own angry memory of the manner in which Sadducees rejected Pharisaic authority.

The Sadducean rejection of the Pharisaic claim is hardly difficult to comprehend. The sage was not a charismatic leader. He did not enhance his authority through ecstacies, prophecy, or miracles. Nor was he a sacerdotal figure. His authority did not rest on either inherited privilege or acquired sanctity. He could not claim authority by reason of a legitimate place in the cult. He did not have any function in the Temple service which might support his demand to direct and interpret the rites. On the contrary, the sage's only authentication was his teaching and his own embodiment of the burden of his message. He represented a third force in religion, opposed to the two primary elements of charisma and traditional routine. These two elements were united in the experience of "Torah." Study of Torah meant to the sages the act of continuing learning in, and application of, Scripture, as at once a fluid and open yet restraining spiritual experience. This was the third way in religion, advanced by the sages as an alternative to Galilee's faith in intimacy with God and to Jerusalem's routine of cultic technology.

Before the destruction of the Temple, the sages had only one opportunity to effect their practical policies through political means. This occurred during the reign of Agrippa I (A.D., 41-44), Herod's grandson, Agrippa entered the Pharisaic imagination as a good king. Though he seems to have presented himself as a Greek to the Caesarean Greeks, in Jerusalem, at least, he behaved like a loyal Jew and prince of Israel. There he observed the commandments just as the Pharisees taught him. On one occasion he took part in a public reading of the Scriptures, receiving the scrolls while standing although it was permissible to sit. He even read standing and thereby won further praise of the sages. When he came to the verse "You must not set a foreigner over you, one who is not your kinsman" (Deut. 17:15), Agrippa, heir to Edomites, burst into tears. The sages called out to him, "You are our brother, you are our brother." Agrippa intended to free the nation from foreign domination. For this reason he cultivated the Pharisaic leaders to win additional popular support. He began to construct a strong wall for the city. He called a meeting of neighboring vassal kings in Tiberias. But the Roman legate in Syria forbade the first and dismissed the second. He died of some kind of stroke before his plans could be tried. His son, aged seventeen, remained in retirement. The land returned to the direct authority of the Roman procurators. Under the subsequent authorities public order apparently declined.

The sages perceived omens of coming disaster. But their political impotence prevented their taking effective remedial action. Yohanan ben Zakkai was reported to have witnessed and interpreted such an omen. Forty years before the destruction of the Temple, the doors of the sanctuary opened by themselves. Rabban Yohanan ben Zakkai thereupon rebuked them: "He said: 'Oh Temple! Temple! Why do you yourself give the alarm? I know about you that you will be destroyed, for Zechariah ben Iddo has already prophesied concerning you, Open your doors, O Lebanon, that the fire may consume your cedars' (Zech. 11:1) ." Josephus recorded a similar omen concerning the massive brass eastern gate of the Temple's inner court. Though securely locked by iron bolts, the gate opened by itself in the middle of the night. The watchman of the Temple ran and reported the matter to the captain. He came up and with difficulty succeeded in shutting it. If Josephus' account is historical, then one would assume that the story about Yohanan was intended to provide a Pharisaic replica of the same curious event. A long time before the destruction the sage was able to foresee its imminence by correctly interpreting events in the light of Scripture in reference to Scriptural passages on *Lebanon*.

iii. The Jerusalem Pharisees

If, whatever their prescience, the Pharisees were unable to prevent the collapse of the social order, they nonetheless continued to evolve their own ideas about the proper conduct of society according to the biblical imperative. They pursued their studies and attempted to apply their insights to public life. They were under the authority of Gamaliel I, who represented them in the Sanhedrin. Gamaliel, like Hillel before him and Yohanan afterward, issued several legal edicts for "the repair of the world," touching upon matters of family law and the sacred calendar. Gamaliel's authority probably was accepted by some Jews throughout the land and in the exilic communities, but we do not know how many, or why they did so. Some of his pastoral letters to other parts of the country and to the Diaspora survive. One of them was as follows:

> It once happened that Rabban Gamaliel was sitting on the stairway of the Temple mount, and Yohanan the scribe was standing before him with three letters prepared.
>
> He said to him, "Take one letter and write, 'To our brothers, men of the lower Galilee, may your peace increase! We beg to inform you that the time of removal has arrived, to remove the tithes from the olive heaps.' "
>
> "Take another letter and write, 'To our brothers, men of the South, may your peace increase! We beg to inform you that the time of removal has arrived, and to separate the tithes from the sheaves of wheat.' "
>
> "And take the last letter and write, 'To our brothers, Men of the Exile in Babylon, and to our brothers in Media, and to the rest of the whole Exile of Israel, may your peace increase for ever! We beg to inform you that the pigeons are yet tender, and the lambs weak, and the springtide has not yet come, and the matter seems fit in my eyes and in the eyes of my colleagues, and I have added to this year thirty days.' "

After the death of Gamaliel I, Simeon ben Gamaliel and Yohanan ben Zakkai continued to send such pastoral letters. The record of one is as follows:

> Rabbi Joshua reported, "Once I went to the Upper Market, to the Refuse Gate in Jerusalem, and I found there Rabban Simeon ben Gamaliel and Rabban Yohanan ben Zakkai, sitting with two scrolls open before them. Yohanan the Scribe was standing before them with pen and ink in his hand."

They said, "Write: 'From Simeon ben Gamaliel and from Yoḥanan ben Zakkai, to our brothers in the Upper and Lower South, and to Shaḥlil, and to the Seven Cities of the South, Peace! Let it be known to you that the fourth year has arrived, but still the sacred produce has not been removed. But now, haste and bring five sheaves, for they hinder the Confession; and it is not we who have begun to write to you, but our fathers used to write to your fathers.' "

"They said to him, Write a second letter, 'From Simeon ben Gamaliel and from Yoḥanan ben Zakkai to our brothers in the Upper and Lower Galilee, and to Simonia, and to 'Oved Bet Hillel, Peace! Let it be known to you that the fourth year has arrived, but still the sacred produce has not been removed. But now, make haste and bring of the olive heaps, for they hinder the Confession; and it is not we who have begun to write to you, but our fathers used to write to your fathers.' "

Besides his son Simeon, Gamaliel I left a daughter, whose daughter married Yoḥanan's student Simon ben Natanel, the priest. When he died, it was said, "the honor of Torah ceased, and purity and separateness passed away." Simeon ben Gamaliel also issued special decrees, particularly to improve the position of women. He was a juggler, and with "gifts of intelligence and judgment, he could by sheer genius retrieve an unfortunate situation in affairs of state." He led the prowar faction of the Pharisees during the revolution and held authority in the first coalition government. It was rumored that he died at the hands of the Romans, but this is by no means certain.

Why Simeon ben Gamaliel shared the headship with Yoḥanan is not clear. The system of joint tenure ("the pairs") of leadership, which apparently ended with the appointment of Hillel's son, now was resumed. Perhaps dissatisfaction with the domination of the Hillelite dynasty led to the return to the old way. If so, however, as soon as the Hillelites could manage it—that is, when Gamaliel II came to power upon Yoḥanan ben Zakkai's retirement—they ceased to share with anyone else the headship of the Pharisaic group and treated the patriarchate as a hereditary right. Why Yoḥanan in particular was chosen to share with Simeon the position of leadership is no clearer. Nothing in the record available to us suggests that he was particularly successful as a political and sectarian leader. All the stories of his excellence as Hillel's student come later. They obviously reflect the viewpoint of those critical of the Hillelite dynasty. These stories omit all reference to Gamaliel I. They stress that Yoḥanan, the youngest of the students, proved worthy of the succession—and do not mention Hillel's own son! Later tradents thus intended a criticism of the hereditary system of succession. While everyone knew that Gamaliel I had actually succeeded, it was Yoḥanan who really "took over from Hillel and Shamai." Yoḥanan was *the* outstanding student. For this reason he was the true successor. Gamaliel I was passed over in silence. So too, the tradents imply, knowledge of Torah, and *not* descent from Hillel (and David), should always determine the succession.

But that does not help us to understand how it came to pass that Simeon ben Gamaliel by himself did not succeed his father. Yoḥanan's distinction in mastering and teaching the traditions must have won him considerable reputation in the party. In the eyes of many he surely appeared to be the most learned and distinguished master of Torah of the day. When Gamaliel I died, it may, therefore, have seemed appropriate to everyone to appoint Yoḥanan as well as Gamaliel's son.

One cannot, however, ignore other more worldly possibilities. Perhaps political or legal issues divided the party, so it had split into contending groups. In order to preserve unity leaders of the divisions would have shared office. We cannot speculate on disputes over legal policies, for the record of Yoḥanan's legal teachings before 70, like that of Simeon ben Gamaliel, is too sparse to permit any sort of conjecture. But a political issue may have proved consequential. In 66, Simeon ben Gamaliel took a place in the revolutionary council, while Yoḥanan did not. In fact, Josephus fails to mention Yoḥanan at all. If the Pharisees were divided into those favoring militant anti-Roman action and those advocating a policy of nonresistance, Yoḥanan obviously would have led the latter group, and Simeon, the former one. As we shall see, Yoḥanan's comment on the antipagan riots in Yavneh in A.D. 40 makes it clear that he had earlier opposed the Zealots' policies. Simeon's acceptability to the revolutionary council suggests that he by no means rejected Zealotry. So the divided leadership may indicate that the Pharisees were not of one mind on the vexed issue of policy toward Rome. Yoḥanan's inclusion would, therefore, have been meant to satisfy the pacifist wing. This is, however, pure conjecture. What is not conjectural is the high esteem in which Yoḥanan was held by some, perhaps many, sages. I have noted that Yoḥanan was not a worldly success. As we shall see, before 66, the priests did not obey him. When war threatened, he was powerless to avert it. He had no influence in the revolutionary councils, and he was ignored by the generals. His leadership proved ineffectual, but his prestige within the Pharisaic community, his reputation as a master of Torah, his teaching of important disciples—these testify to another kind of achievement.

Though the sages had to work in order to keep from starving, the schools were crowded. Yoḥanan conducted one such academy, which neither had a rigid curriculum (after certain fundamentals were mastered) nor even conferred a formally recognized degree. The academy did not have its own building, for the stairway leading to the Temple mount, on the westward side of the Offal Gate, was the place where Yoḥanan sat and lectured to his students. The Temple area, like others in the classical world, was used as a place for public instruction. The Essene master, Judah, had taught there earlier, as had Jesus of Nazareth. Yoḥanan did not use the courts of the Temple. He sat in the shadow of the Temple, where he could see it. The Temple was one of the wonders of the ancient world. "He who has not seen Herod's building has never in his life seen a beautiful building," a saying went. It provided an appropriate setting for Yoḥanan's teaching of Torah.

iv. Yoḥanan and the Sons of the High Priests

The priests contended that they had the right to rule on legal matters as well as Temple rites, and Yoḥanan opposed their decisions in two known cases. The priestly decisions were handed down by the "sons of the high priests," in competition, apparently, with the municipal courts which judged cases of civil law and commercial transactions. Yoḥanan supported the decisions of the municipal justice in two cases dealing with women's rights. "If a man went beyond the sea, and his wife claimed maintenance, Ḥanan said, 'Let her swear [to her claim] at the end of the time, and let her not swear at the beginning.' " That is, when the woman comes to claim her marriage-money—if her husband died, or if he returns and claims that he left her funds for her own maintenance— she must take an oath that she has not held back any of her husband's property. Ḥanan ruled that she need not take a presumptive (*propter hoc*) oath, but is required to swear only at the end of the period in question. To this, the "sons of the high priests" said: "Let her swear when she makes claim for maintenance as well as when she claims what is due her as marriage money."

Yoḥanan ben Zakkai ruled: "Ḥanan has spoken well. Let her swear only at the end."

In the second case, the same pattern recurred: "If a man went beyond the sea and another maintained his wife, Ḥanan said, 'The second has lost his money.' But the sons of the high priests disputed with him, and said, 'Let him swear on oath how much he has expended, and let him recover it.' Rabban Yoḥanan ben Zakkai said: 'Ḥanan has spoken well; he has laid his money on the horn of a gazelle.' " The "sons of the high (or important) priests," equivalent to the sages' court, regulated the affairs of those who adhered to their viewpoint, levied twice the normal marriage-money for the daughters of the high priests, communicated with Diaspora communities, and tried men charged with the violation of Temple laws. They also calculated a calendar of their own, employing rules of evidence different from those of the sages. The two groups clearly differed on the position of the wife in relation to her husband's authority and on the measure of control of the husband's property to be entrusted to the wife. It may well have been that the sages opposed unnecessary oaths, preferring to provide the woman an income without adjuration until the final accounting.

Yoḥanan also criticized the upper classes for "neglect of Torah" and warned that children must be kept away from commercial life and brought to the academies:

> "Keep the children away from the proud, and separate them from the householders, because the householders draw a man far from words of Torah."
>
> He used to say, "For three [sic] kinds of sins, householders are given over to the Government: because they lend money on interest, because they preserve mortgages which have already been paid, because they promise publicly to give charity and do not give, and because they remove from themselves the yoke of taxes and place it on the poor, the needy, and the oppressed, and concerning them it is written, *Cursed is he who will not fulfil the words of this Torah* (Deut. 27:26) —these are the householders."

In this saying, the "proud" clearly refers to the upper classes, and Yoḥanan was warning against the pernicious influence of business on the education of the youth.

v. Yoḥanan and the Temple Councillor

Yoḥanan, as a leading Pharisee, came into conflict with other Temple officials:

> Simon of Sikhnin, the Councillor, Supervisor of the Water Supply, said to Yoḥanan ben Zakkai, "I am as great as you." Yoḥanan asked, "Why?"
>
> "Because I, like you, am occupied with the public welfare." Yoḥanan said to him, "But if someone comes to you for a legal decision or for information, what will you say to him? Will you say, 'Drink from this cistern, for its waters are pure and cold'? Or if a woman comes with a question of ritual uncleanness, will you say to her, 'Dip yourself in this cistern, for its waters purify'?" [Cistern waters cannot purify.]
>
> And of this man, Yoḥanan spoke the verse (Eccles. 5:1), *Guard your steps when you go to the house of God. To draw*

*near to listen is better than to offer sacrifice of fools, for they
do not know they are doing evil.*

Simon's exact title was "Councilman, Digger of Trenches, Cisterns, and Pools." Among the Temple officers, one is listed as a trench digger and defined elsewhere as a man who knew which rocks were likely to yield water. Simon of Sikhnin, the Councilman, was therefore a Temple authority. A water diviner, or "digger of wells, cisterns, and pools in Jerusalem" held an important responsibility. The water supply throughout this period was superb and withstood the exigencies of siege. Yoḥanan nonetheless professed to regard his own capacities as still more significant. To offer Torah, here comprehending both justice and ritual law, is a greater service than providing pure water, no matter how sophisticated the technology of sanitation.

vi. Yoḥanan and the Sadducees

Yoḥanan's main antagonists in Jerusalem were not the wealthy men as such. Some leading citizens attended festal gatherings in his academy. He witnessed the marriage contracts for the richest daughters of the city. Nor was he hostile to all members of the priestly classes on account of their sacerdotal privileges, for he counted among his students priests as well as laity. His principal struggle was with the Sadducean party. In these encounters, he supposedly acted as spokesman for the Pharisees. Each of the extant disputes centered about a petty, sometimes esoteric issue of law, usually of ritual cleanness and uncleanness. Yet we must be aware of the possibly broader matters at issue in the relatively narrow terms of argument. The apparently minor argument on whether Holy Scriptures have the capacity to render the hands unclean or not, for instance, may have represented the Pharisaic assertion phrased in ritual and legal terms that study was equivalent to sacrifice:

> The Sadducees say, "We cry out against you, O Pharisees, for you say the Holy Scriptures render the hands unclean and the books of Homer do not render the hands unclean."

Rabban Yoḥanan ben Zakkai said, "And have we nothing but this against the Pharisees? For lo, they say the bones of an ass are pure, but the bones of Yoḥanan the High Priest [John Hyrcanus] are unclean."

They said to him, "As is our love for them, so is their uncleanness, so that no man may make spoons out of the bones of his father and mother."

He said to them, "Even so the Holy Scriptures—as is our love for them, so is their uncleanness, whereas the writings of Homer, which are held in no account, do not render the hands unclean."

The issue at hand was whether one had to wash his hands after touching the sacred Scriptures as the priest had to wash his hands after priestly rites. The Sadducees underlined an apparent anomaly. The Pharisees seemed to have greater reverence for the books of Homer, touching which would not render one's hands unclean, than for the Scriptures which Pharisaism held to be a source of impurity. Yoḥanan replied that the same anomaly applies elsewhere. The bones of human beings—even of a high priest of the Hasmonean dynasty—were likewise a source of impurity, while those of an ass were not. The Sadducean answer was reasonable: If bones are unclean, people will not make profane use of them. Yoḥanan shared this reasoning: What is a source of uncleanness will not be casually handled or tossed about. The parchment of a sacred scroll must be a source of uncleanness so as to protect it. The Sadducees ruled in the Temple, so even the Pharisaic rule was that the Torah Scroll of the sanctuary does not defile the hands. But outside the sanctuary the Pharisaic rule on the uncleanness of Scriptures applied in their circles. The sage thus asserted service of God through the study of Torah merited the same sacred devotion as that of the priest in the Temple. This idea found expression in later literature as follows:

Whoever busies himself in Torah needs neither burnt-offering nor sin offering.

Whoever busies himself in Torah—it is as if he offered a burnt-offering.

A second argument in a minor detail of the law of cleanness likewise concealed a more important principle. In order to understand the dispute at hand, we must have in mind how troublesome the laws of purity were for the Jerusalem tradesman and worker who prepared produce for use in the sacrificial service. In order to keep his ware fit for the Temple, the worker had to remain in a state of ritual purity. Furthermore, many Jerusalemite workers ate the second tithe, which was brought from round about to be consumed in Jerusalem. They had to remain pure for that purpose. On the other hand, the rural populace rarely obeyed such laws. The priests who spent considerable time in the Temple found it easy to avoid ritual contamination. Thus, the lower and middle classes bore the burden of the purity laws. The Pharisees, legislating in their behalf, tried to ease this burden.

One of their most important enactments was to declare that when a man had bathed after becoming unclean from a major impurity, he remained unclean until evening in accordance with Scripture, *but* not in the original degree of impurity. His degree of impurity was diminished so that he himself would not *impart* impurity to household utensils. Thus, he was able to go about his work. He was only barred from the Temple. This was the *tevul-yom*, a man who has bathed from impurity, but had not yet finished out the day of Levitical uncleanness. The Pharisaic legislation, however, was rejected by Sadducean party who wished to maintain the full stringency of the laws of uncleanness for the entire period and would not recognize that bathing had diminished it in the slightest.

One occasion, apart from the paschal sacrifice, provided an opportunity to advance this viewpoint in action—a sacrificial ceremony which took place *outside* the sanctuary. The burning of the red heifer to create purification ashes took place not in the sanctuary, but on the Mount of Olives. The ceremony would not require absolute purity. If the Sadducean priests there observed a more stringent ruling, they would thus manifest rejection of the Pharisaic ruling. Later Pharisaic tradition had no reliable information on the sacrifice of the cows, but it preserved various, mutually contradictory stories about high priests forced to conform to the Pharisaic viewpoint and even credited Yoḥanan ben Zakkai with having defiled one right in the midst of the ceremonies, to prevent its completion in Sadducean purity.

The Pharisees related that the ceremony took place only seven times in the entire history of the Second Commonwealth:

> "Who had prepared them? Moses prepared the first, Ezra prepared the second, and five were prepared after Ezra," so Rabbi Meir.
>
> But the sages say, "Seven since Ezra. And who prepared them? Simon the Just and Yoḥanan the High Priest prepared two each, and Elyehoenai the son of Hakkof (Caiaphas), Ḥanamel the Egyptian, and Ishmael the son of Phiabi prepared one each."

The Mount of Olives contained a place of immersion, and the high priest was rendered unclean "because of the Sadducees, that they should not be able to say, 'It must be performed only by one on whom the sun has set.' They laid their hands upon him and said, 'My Lord, high priest, immerse thyself this once.' He went down, immersed himself, came up, dried himself." Then, as a *ṭevul-yom,* the high priest supposedly slaughtered the cow and burned its ashes.

The following account included Yoḥanan ben Zakkai:

> It once happened that a certain Sadducee waited out the night of his uncleanness and came to burn the red heifer. Rabban Yoḥanan ben Zakkai heard of the matter, and placed his two hands on him, rendering him unclean again, and said to him, "My lord high priest, how fitting it is for you to be high priest! Now go, immerse."
>
> The man went and immersed, and came back. When he came up, he slit his ear [thereby rendering him unfit for the priestly service], and the priest said to Yoḥanan, "Ben Zakkai—when I have time to deal with you . . . ."

"If you have time," he replied.

Three days did not pass before they buried him, and his father came to Yoḥanan and said, "My son has time."

Since the traditions deal here with Yoḥanan ben Zakkai and an unnamed high priest, and since Ishmael ben Phiabi was a contemporary, some have thought that Yoḥanan's encounter was with him. But this is manifestly impossible for it was also recorded that Ishmael ben Phiabi *did* accept the sages' authority. One could scarcely harmonize such a tradition with his sudden death on Yoḥanan's account. Furthermore, Ishmael was remembered with high regard: "When *Rabbi* [sic] Ishmael ben Phiabi died, the splendor of the priesthood ceased."

If the incident did not happen with Ishmael, however, it is difficult to explain, for no other high priest is known to have officiated or attempted to officiate at the heifer ceremony during Yoḥanan's lifetime. Ḥanamel was high priest under Herod. Since the sources so clearly conflict, one must conclude that the editors of the Mishnah and Tosefta had no reliable information whatever on the subject. The Pharisaic position which Yoḥanan was said to have advanced even with violence certainly favored the interest of the urban populace who would have found it difficult to cope with the laws of purity if they, defiled almost daily from some source of contamination, could render unclean by a slight touch every object around them. The Pharisaic rule also encouraged the custom of bathing in a ritual pool each morning, a measure that contributed to hygienic purity in the crowded city.

What is the deeper meaning of this dispute? It was simple and self-evident to the priests. The Pharisees, led by Yoḥanan ben Zakkai, were attempting not merely to rule the sanctuary, but to *exclude* from the Temple all who did not accept their rulings. To appreciate the effrontery of the rabbis, we must recall that the Sadducees probably regarded themselves as direct heirs of the line of Ẓaddoq. Sadducean myth held that King David had entrusted Ẓaddoq, their very ancestor, with the Temple cult. For close to ten centuries their fathers had kept the Temple and offered up its sacrifices to a gracious God. The issues of law, even to make life easier for Jerusalem's lower classes, therefore mattered far less than a very striking partisan claim of the Pharisees. They would have rendered unfit and profane not merely the Sadducees of the first century, but *all* that had been said and done in the Temple for nearly a thousand years. Whatever had not been done in the Pharisaic manner was thereby to be declared profane. Not only to be excluded from the Temple, but also to be forced to repudiate the rightful actions of so many generations of their forefathers—these were no light matters. The Temple authorities did not take them lightly. Indeed, like the colloquy with Simon of Sikhnin, the supposed incident at the burning of the cow must be understood as a mere skirmish in a larger struggle over the Temple, present, past, and future.

The fight was for the Temple's spiritual influence over Jewry in Palestine and throughout the Diaspora as well. Jews from far and wide made pilgrimages to Jerusalem *not* to study in the rabbinical academies, but to offer sacrifices in the holy Temple. The messages which they brought home with them came from the priesthood. The letters they received, similarly, came from Temple officials. From the perspective of A.D. 50, the disputes entailed more than recognition of "study of Torah" as equivalent to Temple cult, but rather, Who would control the Temple? And who would thereby direct the spiritual life of the Jewish people from Medea and Babylonia in the east to Tunisia and Italy in the west? The Pharisees could hardly have foreseen their ultimate triumph. Whatever Yoḥanan's prescience, they like other Jews knew the lesson of Scripture. Once before the Temple had been destroyed "on account of idolatry." The people, having purged themselves of their sin through exile and suffering, never repeated that sin. Hence, it could hardly be predicted that the Temple would lie in ruins in just a few years. No one knew that the Sadducees would soon be scattered, bereft of their base of power and influence over the country and beyond. None suspected that the Essenes and Zealots would be wiped out, and that the Romans would turn to the Pharisees to govern. Without such foreknowledge, all that the Pharisees of the mid-first century could have known was that the Temple provided the sole battleground. Exegesis of law and of Scripture was their only weapon in the struggle. So we understand the echoes of ancient bitterness and the recurring struggles over points of law which retrospectively seem hardly worth the fight.

vii. The Priests' Response to Yoḥanan

For their part, the Temple authorities and councillors, Sadducees, and priests did not leave records of their opinions of Yoḥanan and his colleagues, but we may be certain that they ignored his viewpoint. Yoḥanan and his associates claimed to determine who may or may not marry a priest, for families of impure lineage were denied that right. Yoḥanan's viewpoint was that certain families, excluded by the more strict rules of the priests, in fact were permitted to marry into the priesthood. The priests rejected the Pharisaic leniencies and avoided marriage to such families. In despair, Yoḥanan was reported to have prohibited calling court sessions on such questions. Gamaliel II reported in Yavneh after the destruction:

> Rabbi Joshua and Rabbi Judah ben Bathyra [the former was Yoḥanan's student] testified that the widow of one who belonged to an *'Isah* family [a family suspected of having doubtful stock] was eligible for marriage with a priest, and that the members of such a family were qualified to bear testimony about which of themselves is clean or unclean [in lineage], and which must be put away, and which may be brought near.
>
> Rabban Gamaliel said, "We should accept your testimony, but what shall we do? For Rabban Yoḥanan ben Zakkai decreed that courts may not be called into session concerning this matter. The priests would listen to you in what concerns putting away, but not in what concerns bringing near [to marry into the priesthood]."

Another such case in which the priests refused to accept the sages' judgment involved one of Yoḥanan's students:

Rabbi Yosi the Priest and Rabbi Zechariah son of the Butcher testified concerning a young girl who was left as a pledge in Ashkelon, that the members of her family kept her far from them [that is, the eligible bachelors refused to marry her], although she had witnesses who testified that she had not been closeted with any man, and thereby been defiled.

The sages said to them, "If you believe that she was left as a pledge, believe also that she had not . . . been defiled, but if you do not believe that she had not gone aside and been defiled, do not believe that she has been left as a pledge."

Yoḥanan felt bitterness against the priests who took such strict measures to preserve their family purity, and said that Elijah the prophet, who would come to herald the messiah and to solve all kinds of insoluble problems, would concern himself first and foremost with righting the wrongs committed by the priests. Joshua reported:

I have received as a tradition from Rabban Yoḥanan ben Zakkai, who heard it from his master, and his master from his, as a law given to Moses on Sinai, that Elijah will not come to declare clean or unclean, to remove afar or bring near, but only to remove afar those that have been brought near by violence, and to bring near those that were removed far away by violence.

What is the point of Yoḥanan's saying? Elijah would come to announce the advent of the Messiah, to prepare the way. What would he actually have to do? Yoḥanan held that his chief task would be to set right the injustices committed by the highhanded priests. They ignored the traditions of the Pharisees. They on their own decided questions of legitimacy and genealogical purity. "So-and-so may be married to a priest, and so-and-so may not." And they used force to carry out their word. Since it was a matter of considerable practical benefit to be a priest, more than family pride was involved. Priests received rich tithes and offerings. Yoḥanan felt so bitter about the entire matter that he said the Messianic era could not come before Elijah had set things straight. If the saying of Joshua referred to the period after the Temple's destruction, then a further complaint is to be inferred. The Temple lay in ruins, and it was only Elijah and the Messiah who would in time restore it. But before they could do so, they would *still* have to repair the wrongs committed by the priests. They must first purify the priesthood, which would then minister in the restored sanctuary.

Another way in which the priests ignored the sages' rules was by refusing to pay the sheqel to the Temple. Yohanan interpreted Scripture (Exod. 30:13) to mean that the priests were included in the commandment to support the Temple: "Each who is numbered in the census shall give this: half a sheqel according to the sheqel of the sanctuary" meaning, "all twelve tribes." But, it was taught:

> They did not exact pledges from the priests in the interests of peace. Rabbi Judah said, "Ben Bukhri testified at Yavneh that if a priest paid the sheqel, he did not sin."
>
> Rabban Yohanan ben Zakkai answered, "Not so, but if a priest did *not* pay the sheqel, he committed sin, but the priests used to expound this scripture to their advantage, *And every meal offering of the priest shall be wholly burnt, it shall not be eaten* (Lev. 6:23). Since the 'omer and the two loaves and the showbread are ours how can they be eaten [if we have contributed to their cost]?"

That is to say, since these meal offerings were brought as charges on the Temple funds, the priests could not contribute, for if they did, the offerings would have to be burned ("every meal offering of the priest shall be wholly burned"), and this would be contrary to Scripture itself. The Pharisees had no monopoly on clever exegetes.

Some have surmised that Yohanan ben Zakkai himself was a priest, but the evidence of this is rather scanty. Even if he were a priest, he never participated in the cult, never on this account mitigated his opposition to the priesthood's excessive claims, and never received from the priests any enhanced respect on account of his alleged ancestry.

viii. Yohanan and the Cult

No less than the Temple authorities, Sadducees, and priests, Yohanan and his colleagues were concerned with the welfare of Jerusalem. It was reported of Yohanan that he prayed and fasted for rain as local authorities among the Pharisees had done for generations. It was said that once when he looked forward to rain, he observed the rules of fasting which applied to community authorities, refraining from having his hair cut. Finally he said to his barber, "Stand up before the Temple and say, "My master is grieved because he wants to have his hair cut and must not do so' "—and immediately, the rains came. As an authority in the city, Yohanan was supposed to have used his power to annul ancient rites in the Temple on the pretext that the troubled times rendered them no longer applicable. Later Pharisaic tradition represented him as abrogating the rite of the heifer sacrificed as in the case to which Zaddoq referred, where the murderer was unknown, and also the rite of the waters of cursing, applied to determine whether a woman suspected of infidelity was guilty or not: "When the adulterers increased, the waters of cursing ended and Rabban Yohanan ben Zakkai ended them, as it is said, "I will not visit upon your daughters when they go awhoring" (Hos. 4:14). A second more reliable tradition was that Yohanan ben Zakkai merely reported the cessation of these rites, probably because they fell into desuetude. It is anachronistic to exaggerate his power as "critic" of the Temple rites.

Yohanan, moreover, taught his students that the purification ceremonies had no *ex opere operato* efficacy, but provided merely an additional means to fulfill the will of God as it had been revealed to Moses. Thus, a pagan said to him (perhaps after someone burned a red heifer in the 60's, if, indeed, anyone did) :

> "These deeds which you do look to me like hocus pocus. You bring a heifer and burn it, and crush it, and take its ashes, and if one of you is defiled by a dead corpse, you sprinkle him on

the third and seventh day of his uncleanness, and say to him, 'You are purified.' "

He answered, "Has a wandering spirit ever entered into you?"

"No."

"But have you ever seen a man into whom a wandering spirit ever entered?"

"Yes."

"And what did you do for him?"

"You put smoking roots under him, and throw water over him, and the spirit flees."

He said, "Listen then with your ears to what your mouth speaks! This is a spirit of uncleanness, as we learn in Zechariah (13:2), *And also I shall cause the spirit of uncleanness to pass away from the earth.* You sprinkle on him waters of purification, and it flees."

After the man left, the disciples said to Yohanan, "Master, this man you have driven off with a broken reed. What will you reply to us?"

He answered, "By your lives! It is not the corpse that renders a man unclean, nor the waters which purify, but the Holy One said, 'A statute have I enacted, an ordinance have I ordained, and you are not permitted to transgress my commandment' as it is said [with reference to the heifer], *This is the ordinance of the Torah* (Num. 19:2)."

If this report is true, neither Yohanan nor his students believed that a corpse truly caused substantial uncleanness, or that the sprinkling of the heifer's ashes and water purified. They nonetheless disputed with the officiating priests who did not follow their instructions precisely. In the end, however, they offered only one rationale for such ceremonies: to do them was a part of God's will.

ix. Conclusion

The will of God for man was to be found in the Torah. Yohanan said that the study of Torah was as sacred as the cultic rite. Indeed, after many generations, the destruction of the Temple and the burning of the academy of Yohanan ben Zakkai were mourned with equal lamentation:

Rabbi Joshua ben Levi (3rd c.) said: *"And he burned the house of God* (II Kings 25:9)—this is the Temple. *And the house of the king*—this is the palace of Zedekiah. *And all the houses of Jerusalem*—these are the four hundred and eighty synagogues that were in Jerusalem. *And every great house he burned in flames*—this refers to the academy of Rabban Yoḥanan ben Zakkai, for there they would rehearse the great deeds of the Holy One, blessed be He."

I can think of no more striking expression of the Pharisaic viewpoint. The destruction of the Temple was no more grievous than the burning of the "great house" of Rabban Yoḥanan's academy. The act of study, no less than the act of sacrifice, drew man close to God, but in a better way. Study engaged not merely his agent, the priest, but through learning man himself entered into a direct and personal confrontation with the word of the Creator.

On the eve of 66, Yoḥanan ben Zakkai, now approaching old age, could look back upon a life of struggle with little real accomplishment. For the quarter century after A.D. 40, he had taken a leading role in the Pharisaic party. He predicted that the Temple would be destroyed, but like his prediction of a similar fate for the Galileans, nothing had come of it. The prophecy was merely an expression of resentment. Galilee was not in chains. The Temple was standing as firm and secure as ever. Nothing had changed—but Yoḥanan had grown old. The priests were no better after twenty-five years of Yoḥanan's criticism than before. Simeon of Sikhnin could boast as certainly in 65 as in 40, "I am as great as you." The sons of the high priests were still sending their letters to the Diaspora, still ignoring the sages' judgments. The priests continued to refrain from washing their hands after touching the Holy Scrolls, to wait out the evening of their uncleanness, to celebrate the Pentecost on a Sunday, to divide legacies as they saw fit, and to take exactly what they wanted of the Temple offerings. They did not marry into families regarded as of pure priestly origin by the rabbis. They did not contribute *sheqels* to the Temple. They did believe, unlike Yoḥanan, that the rite of the heifer truly rendered an unclean man clean. The "ordinance of the Torah" reflected actualities, not merely spiritual exercises and disciplines of a ritualistic sort.

What, therefore, can have sustained Yoḥanan, a vigorous exponent of his party's views and violent opponent of the foe? All about him he saw the prosperity of those he thought to be iniquitous or at least in error. We now turn aside from our narrative to reflect upon the inner life of the Torah. We want to uncover the resources which sustained Yoḥanan through his decades of slight success and deep despair. Yoḥanan's inner life is hardly reflected in the political and sectarian disputes we have here considered. That was the outer man, the politician and the partisan. He cursed his foes and rallied his party. He called this one a fool and brutally made the other ineligible for the priesthood. If all we knew of Yoḥanan ben Zakkai were about his partisan life, we should surely wonder what had become of the disciple of Hillel? Could one who *fought* the sons of Aaron be a true "disciple of Aaron"? Where is the love of peace and the love of humanity; where is the patience, the good-heartedness of the master? We have met Yoḥanan's enemies. Who were his friends? We know he was a master of Torah. What were his teachings?

PART TWO:
SOCIETY & SCRIPTURE
IV. Father of Wisdom: The Disciples

i. Introduction

Disciples were not students who came to a master only to learn facts or holy traditions. They came to study the master as well as what the master said. "Torah" was revealed in traditions handed on both orally and in writing. Just as one studied what was written, so he also had to imitate what was not written, but living in the master himself. A living Torah, his every gesture must have some basis in the ancient traditions. The disciple lived with the master because daily life, like classroom discourse, was a school for Torah.

The disciple, indeed, acquired more than a master. He gained a new father. According to later tradition if the disciple had a choice of serving his father or his master, his master took precedence. If he saw his father's and his master's asses stumble at the same time, he had to help his master's, then his father's. The father had brought him into this world, but the master would show him the way to eternal life. The father had given him the life of the hour, but the master would give him the world to come. The master was not merely a surrogate father, taking over a psychological role the father had formerly played. The master was truly and really the second father of the disciple, who would shape him for eternity as the father had for this world. The father had given the physical features. The master would sculpt the soul.

Entry into the rabbinical circle, like initiation into a mystery cult, marked the end of an old existence, the beginning of a new life, a new being. The disciple did not simply learn things; he was converted from one way of living to another.

That new way of living was interpreted by those who lived it in terms of a vivid and all-embracing myth, the "Torah-myth" derived from Pharisaic teaching about the dual Torah. Moses received a single, complete revelation, but only part of it was written down. The other part was preserved in rabbinical schools from Moses' day to the present. Since Moses was seen as the prototype of the rabbi, he was called "Moses our rabbi." But he followed a model, just as the sages copied the model of Moses "our rabbi." And the model for Moses, the source of rabbinical ways, was God himself who was seen as the archetype. God did the things rabbis were supposed to do, and that was why rabbis ought to do them. He studied Torah, donned phylacteries, visited the sick, buried the dead, and performed acts of compassion. We see the rabbi's values as projected onto heaven, but to the rabbi, heavenly values were projected onto earth. Indeed, the school on earth corresponded to the school in heaven. A later account illustrates the correspondence between heaven and earth, between heavenly and earthly academies which lay at the center of the Torah-myth:

> R. Abbahu said, "Solomon was asked, 'Who has a place in the world to come?' "
>
> He replied, "He to whom are applied the words, *And before his elders shall be glory*" (Isa. 24:23) . [That is, one honored for his sagacity.]
>
> A similar teaching was made by Joseph b. R. Joshua. He was sick and fell into a trance. [Afterward] his father said to him, "What vision did you see?"
>
> He replied, "I saw a world upside down, the upper below, the lower above."
>
> He [the father] said to him, "You saw a well-regulated world. And in what condition did you see us?"
>
> He replied, "As is our esteem here [below] so it is there. I also heard them saying, 'Happy is he who comes here in full possession of his Torah.' "

The school was thus the earthly reflection of its heavenly counterpart. "Torah" was more than laws and legends. The

master was more than a teacher. The disciple sought something other than mere education. The issues were salvific and
the goal eternity, conquest of "this world" and attainment of
the world to come. Certainty lay in the conviction that God
through Moses "our rabbi" had long ago laid down the way
to heaven, and the path led directly to the schoolhouse door.

ii. Study of Torah as a Life-Style

Besides Ḥanina ben Dosa, we know of only five of Yoḥanan's
disciples, those who formed the center of his circle in Jerusalem. We do not know much about them. What did they
want out of life? They never produced diaries or letters. What
did they do from day to day? We can only surmise that they
spent much of the day with the master, walking with him,
listening to and talking with him. The rest of the day they
meditated upon what they had heard and learned. One thing
we know for certain: the master was master for life. Yoḥanan's
chief disciples remained at his side until he died. Only at
death did they take leave of him and assume the responsibilities of masters themselves. With their master, the disciples
constituted a social group devoted to the study of Torah and,
where possible, to its application to the day-to-day life of
Israel. They brought to Scripture questions which touched
on moral, legal, ethical, and ritual matters. Through study of
Torah they sought guidance on the conduct of daily affairs.
They believed that the crucial and consequential issues of life
were decided in commonplace actions. But the very *act* of
study was itself crucial. The sage spent most of his life in
study, and through such study he taught how to live: "If
you have done much in the study of Torah, do not claim merit
for yourself, for to this end were you created." If Yoḥanan believed that the very purpose of existence was to study Torah,
one understands why he taught that study of Torah may even
preserve life.

It is told that a certain family in Jerusalem used to lose its
male issue at the age of eighteen. They came and told Rabban
Yoḥanan ben Zakkai.

> He said to them, "Perhaps you are of the descendants of Eli, of whom it is written *Behold the days are coming when I will cut off your strength and the strength of your father's house, so that there will not be an old man in your house* (I Samuel 3:31). Go and study Torah, and live."
>
> They went, studied Torah, and lived. So they called their family by the name of Yoḥanan ben Zakkai in his honor.

Yoḥanan here interpreted Scripture, for it is said, "Therefore I swear to the house of Eli that the iniquity of Eli's house shall not be expiated by sacrifice or offering forever" (I Sam. 3:14). Sacrifice and offerings would not save the priestly family, but the study of Torah *would* bring salvation.

The study of Torah provided a focus for religious life distinct from either cultic ritual or charismatic action. The priests thought to do God's will through the Temple rites, the ecstatics by prayer and meditation. Yoḥanan and the other sages did so by memorizing, interpreting, and applying ancient texts.

These texts were believed to contain the secrets of the inner structure of reality. Through them one came to an understanding of the whole of reality and to an apprehension of the divine will in creation. Torah made manifest the universal design and plan for existence:

> Scripture said *The Lord made me as the beginning of his way, the first of his words of old. I was set up from everlasting, from the beginning or even the earth was made* (Prov. 8:22-30).
>
> "When he marked out the foundations of the earth, then I was beside Him, like a master workman. I was daily His delight, rejoicing before him always."
>
> So the Torah speaks, "I was God's instrument. According to the custom of the world when a mortal king builds a palace, he does not build it by his own skill, but with the skill of an architect. And that architect does not build it out of his own head but employs plans and diagrams in order to know how to arrange the chambers and wicket doors. So too the Holy One, blessed be He, looked into the Torah and created the world."

This idea of "Torah" rested on the notion that the world presented an order and regularity. Man might uncover the laws of the world through the study of what God had revealed, the source of insight into the cosmos. In studying Torah, therefore, a man studied the divine architect's plan for life itself. He achieved the possibility of penetrating life's meaning. The study of Torah may have been an act of the intellect, but when Yoḥanan taught that it was to this end that man was created, he manifested more than an intellectual dedication to the exposition of ancient revelation. He proposed a religious program. Though God was transcendent, his word was immanent, and the sage and disciple should serve him through study of that word.

This program was not, of course, Yoḥanan's invention. The ideal of Torah had been held, for example, by Ben Sira three centuries earlier. For Ben Sira, however, the achievement of wisdom depended on having wealth and leisure. It is instructive to note, therefore, how this ideal had become transformed in the intervening centuries from that of the upper-class intellectual to that of the poor sage:

> The wisdom of the scribe depends on the opportunity of leisure,
> And he who has little business may become wise.
>
> > (Ben Sira 39:1-5)

Ben Sira promised that the sage, a kind of magus in his view, would have a great career, appear before rulers, travel far and wide:

> He will serve among great men and appear before rulers
> He will travel through the lands of foreign nations
> For he tests the good and the evil among men.
>
> > (Ben Sira 39:4-5)

Some of the sages, particularly Gamaliel I, Simeon ben Gamaliel, and Josephus, who adhered to the Pharisaic party did pursue public careers. Yoḥanan himself served among the great men of Jerusalem. The sages did not find public careers open to them and did not travel abroad. They were mostly poor. Yoḥanan himself, however, did see the fulfillment of one of Ben Sira's promises:

If he lives long, he will leave a name greater than a thousand. But if he goes to rest, it is enough for him.

(Ben Sira 39:11)

If the sage merited long life, he could hope to leave a lasting monument, but if he died before his time, he could at least say *"Enough! I have had my portion in Torah."* Thus, when his son died, Yoḥanan was comforted to know that his son had done his appointed task.

When Rabban Yoḥanan ben Zakkai's son died, his disciples came to comfort him.

Rabbi Eliezer entered, sat down before him, and said to him, "Master, by your leave, may I say something to you?"

"Speak," he replied.

Rabbi Eliezer said to him, "Adam had a son who died, yet he allowed himself to be comforted concerning him. And how do we know that he allowed himself to be comforted concerning him? For it is said, *And Adam knew his wife again* (Gen. 4:25). You too, be comforted."

Rabbi Yoḥanan said to him, "Is it not enough that I grieve over my own, that you should remind me of the grief of Adam?"

Rabbi Joshua entered and said to him, "Master, by your leave, may I say something to you?"

"Speak," he replied.

Rabbi Joshua said, "Job had sons and daughters, all of whom died on one day. Yet he allowed himself to be comforted concerning them. You too, be comforted. And how do we know that Job was comforted? For it is said, *The Lord gave, and the Lord has taken away. Blessed be the name of the Lord"* (Job 1:21).

Rabban Yoḥanan said to him, "Is it not enough that I grieve over my own, that you remind me of the grief of Job?"

Rabbi Yosi entered and sat down before him. He said to him, "Master, by your leave, may I say something to you?"

"Speak," he replied.

"Aaron had two grown sons," he said, "both of whom died in one day, yet he allowed himself to be comforted for them, as it is said, *And Aaron held his peace* (Lev. 10:3) —and silence is no other than consolation. You too, be comforted."

Rabban Yoḥanan said to him, "Is it not enough that I grieve over my own, that you remind me of the grief of Aaron?"

Rabbi Simeon entered and said to him, "Master, by your leave, may I say something to you?"

"Speak," he replied.

Rabbi Simeon said, "King David had a son who died, yet he allowed himself to be comforted. You too, therefore, be comforted. And how do we know that David was comforted? For it is said, *And David comforted Beth Sheba his wife, and went to her, and lay with her, and she bore a son, and called his name Solomon* (II Sam. 12:24). You too, Master, be comforted."

He replied, "Is it not enough that I grieve over my own son that you remind me of the grief of King David?"

Then Rabbi Eleazar ben Arakh entered.

As soon as Rabban Yoḥanan saw him, he said to his servant, "Take my clothing and follow me to the bath house, for he is a great man, and I shall be unable to resist him."

Rabbi Eleazar entered, sat down before him, and said to him, "I shall tell you a parable. To what may this be likened? To a man with whom the king deposited some object. Every single day the man would weep and cry out, saying, Woe unto me! When shall I complete and fulfil this trust in peace? You too, Master—you had a son, he studied Torah, Prophets, the Holy Writings, he studied Mishnah, *halakhah, aggada,* and he departed from the world without sin. And you should be comforted when you have returned your trust unimpaired."

Rabban Yoḥanan said to him, "Rabbi Eleazar, my son, you have comforted me the way men should give comfort."

When Yoḥanan's son was sick, he was revived by Ḥanina's miracle. When he died in Yoḥanan's middle years, Yoḥanan found comfort in his own conviction that his son had done what he had been created to do.

iii. Torah and Fellowship

The study of Torah yielded more than moral and religious benefits. It also created a community, bringing student and teacher together. Sitting, walking, and traveling the sages speculated together on momentous matters. This fellowship of interested men represented another kind of polity in the urban, lonely, isolated situation. Like the Pharisaic fellowship (havurah), the Nazarene community in Jerusalem, and the monastery at Qumran, it entailed a social commitment. Among these men and in their society, the spiritual life should be lived.

Such a social group was not unique, for the pagan world had long witnessed the formation of societies for the communal study of religious and intellectual problems. Speculative problems, studied by Academic and Peripatetic masters and their disciples, had long ago given way to deepening concern for moral issues. Ancient metaphysical perplexities were left behind. With the end of the corporate life of ancient cities, ancestral laws and institutions lost their cloak of near-divine authority. The moral supports of society, now found to be insecure, became the focus of concern. Indeed, the individual was thrown back upon his own resources. The great problems of philosophy centered upon how to achieve autonomy of character. Not only in the Land of Israel, but throughout the world men had been uprooted from their ancient foundations. The sensitive among them experienced profound alienation. Submerged into the masses of men in the cosmopolitan cities, they lacked adequate expression for their individuality. Those who were able to find new expression for their own souls had to speak to a changing social setting. They needed to provide disciples with a new corporate society to explore the implications of ancient wisdom for daily affairs. The academy thus was both a school for life and at the same time the setting for individual living and for the expression of the private person's individuality. Opportunities for such self-expression were no longer easily available in the common life of the city. The end of the corporate community of the ancient city, in which each man had his place and his hour, created undifferentiated masses. From such masses came men seeking for themselves a means of individual and social expression.

In Rome, uprooted men found for themselves a kind of

spiritual or moral master who would impart the "art of life." Such a moral director was qualified by his profound knowledge of the pathology of the soul. He offered private counsel, much as the analyst does today, for the particular needs of his spiritual patient. He encouraged his charge to "make full confession of the diseases of his soul." He trained him in moral self-examination and tried to help him find the way to right living in a world gone wrong. The goal was to produce the *sapiens,* who was, in the words of Samuel Dill:

> The man who sees in the light of Eternal Reason the true proportions of things, whose affections have been trained to obey the higher law, whose will has hardened into an unswerving conformity to it in all the difficulties of conduct, and the true philosopher is no longer the cold, detached student of intellectual problems far removed from the struggles and miseries of human life. He has become the *generis humani paedagogus,* the schoolmaster to bring men to the Ideal Man.

There could be no more appropriate description of the task assumed by Yoḥanan ben Zakkai and his colleagues, but in characteristically Jewish fashion Yoḥanan found "eternal reason" in the Torah and looked for the "higher law" in ancient revelation. He sought to bring men not to the "Ideal Man," but closer to their Father in Heaven. If Seneca, who was Yoḥanan's contemporary, thought to root character in faith in the rational law of conduct, Yoḥanan saw the foundation of all natural law in the Torah. Both would have agreed that freedom is achieved through conformity to the higher part of being, the vision of which provides universal laws for particular actions. Each tried to create a world in which men might once again matter.

iv. The Disciples

Yoḥanan ben Zakkai had five disciples in his circle in Jerusalêm. For each he had a name:

> Eliezer ben Hyrcanus he called "plastered cistern which loses not a drop, pitch-coated flask, which keeps its wine."

Joshua ben Ḥananiah he called "three-fold cord not quickly broken."

Yosi the Priest he called "the generation's saint."

Simeon ben Nathanel he called "oasis in the desert, which holds onto its water."

And Eleazar ben Arakh he called "overflowing stream and ever-flowing stream whose waters ever flow and overflow—confirming the statement, *Let thy springs be dispersed abroad, and courses of water in the streets*" (Prov. 5:16).

For one, he had very special praise:

He used to say, "If all the sages of Israel were in one scale of the balance, and Rabbi Eliezer ben Hyrcanus were in the other scale, he would outweigh them all."

Abba Shaul said in his name, "If all the sages of Israel were in one scale of the balance, and even if Rabbi Eliezer ben Hyrcanus were with them, and Rabbi Eleazar ben Arakh were in the other scale, *he* would outweigh them all."

Much like the philosophical director in Seneca's Rome, Yoḥanan would discourse with his students on basic questions facing moral man. He sought an ethic applicable to all men and in all places. Yoḥanan asked his students, "What is the good way of life," and "What is the evil way of life," always phrasing his moral inquiries in broad, universal terms. In each case, he demanded observation of life as it was lived, telling his disciples to go out and see the world for themselves.

He told them: "Go out and see which is the good way to which a man should cleave, so that through it he may enter the world to come."

The students returned with their conclusions.

Rabbi Eliezer came in and said, "A good eye [that is, liberality]."

Rabbi Joshua came in and said, "A good companion."

Rabbi Yosi came in and said, "A good neighbor, a good impulse and a good wife."

Rabbi Simeon came in and said, "Foresight."

Rabbi Eleazar came in and said, "Good-heartedness [or cheerfulness] toward heaven, good-heartedness toward the command-ments, and good-heartedness toward mankind."

Rabban Yoḥanan said to them, "I prefer the words of Rabbi Eleazar ben Arakh to your words, for in his words, your words are included."

On another occasion he told his students, "Go out and see which is the evil way which a man should shun, so that he may enter the world to come."

The students again returned.

Rabbi Eliezer said, "An evil eye [that is, avarice]."

Rabbi Joshua came in and said, "An evil companion."

Rabbi Yosi said, "An evil neighbor, and evil impulse, and an evil wife."

Rabbi Simeon said, "Borrowing and not repaying, for he that borrows is as one who borrows from God, as it is said, *The wicked borrows and pays not, but the righteous deals graciously and gives*" (Ps. 37:21).

Rabbi Eleazar said, "Mean-heartedness toward heaven, and mean-heartedness toward the commandments, and mean-heartedness toward mankind."

To this Yoḥanan replied, "I prefer the words of Rabbi Eleazar to your words, for in his words, your words are included."

On this passage, Judah Goldin comments:

The answers of the disciples are far from clear, but if we wish to capture something of the meaning of this exchange be-tween Johanan and his disciples, it is terribly important to listen to his question with utmost attention. Johanan did not ask a trivial question, nor did he express himself carelessly. He asked about the way to which a man should 'cleave,' *dabaq*.

The term *dabaq* . . . is no ordinary term, and it was no ordin-ary question Johanan asked, and the give-and-take with his disciples was no ordinary conversation. The idiom reveals a certain intensiveness, a certain *fervor*, and this is the telling thing. It is the idiom which suddenly summons up remem-brances of a mood and a tone of voice which were current in Hellenist circles. As Nock wrote three decades ago: "This idea [that devotion to philosophy would make a difference in a man's life] was not thought of as a matter of purely intellectual conviction. The philosopher commonly said not 'Follow my arguments one by one, check and control them to the best of you ability; truth should be dearer than Plato to you,' but 'Look at this picture which I paint, and can you resist its attractions? Can you refuse a hearing to the legitimate rhetoric which I address to you in the name of virtue?' Even Epicurus says in an argument, 'Do not be deceived, men, or led astray: do not fall. There is no natural fellowship between reasonable beings. *Believe me,* those who express the other view deceive you and argue you out of what is right.' Epictetus, II, 19, 34 also employs the same appeal, *Believe me,* and counters opponents by arguments which appeal to the heart and not to the head. Inside the schools, at least inside the academic school, there was an atmosphere of hard thinking, of which something survives in the various commentaries on Aristotle. Yet even in the schools this was overcast by tradition and loyalty. . . . The philosophy which addressed itself to the world at large was a dogmatic philosophy seeking to save souls."

Thus, a circle of students came together with Yoḥanan ben Zakkai for the study of moral questions. At least two of them began their education with him, starting from the most elementary duties of religious life. One of these, Simeon ben Natanel, was an ignorant man at the beginning, coming in his mature years from an unlettered family. Yoḥanan therefore called him an "oasis in the desert." The second, Eliezer ben Hyrcanus, also came at a mature age. About his origins we have a full account:

> What were the beginnings of Rabbi Eliezer ben Hyrcanus? He was twenty-two years old, and had not yet studied Torah. One time he resolved, "I will go and study Torah with Rabbi Yoḥanan ben Zakkai."
> His father Hyrcanus said to him, "Not a taste of food shall you get before you have plowed the entire field." He rose early in the morning, plowed the entire field, and then departed for Jerusalem.
> As he was walking along the road, he saw a stone. He picked it up and put it into his mouth. Some say it was cattle dung. He went to spend the night at a hostel.

Then he went and appeared before Rabban Yoḥanan ben Zakkai in Jerusalem. A bad breath rose from his mouth. Said Rabban Yoḥanan ben Zakkai to him, "Eliezer my son, have you eaten at all today?"

Silence.

Rabban Yoḥanan ben Zakkai asked him again.

Silence again.

Rabban Yoḥanan ben Zakkai sent for the owners of his hostel and asked them, "Did Eliezer have anything to eat at your place?"

"We thought," they replied, "he was very likely eating with you."

He said, "And I thought he was very likely eating with you. You and I, between us, left Rabbi Eliezer to perish."

Thereupon Rabban Yoḥanan said to him, "Even as a bad breath rose from your mouth, so shall your fame travel for your mastery of the Torah."

When Hyrcanus his father heard of him that he was studying Torah with Rabban Yoḥanan ben Zakkai, he declared, "I shall go and ban my son Eliezer from my possessions."

That day Rabban Yoḥanan ben Zakkai sat expounding in Jerusalem, and all the great ones of Israel sat before him. When he heard that Hyrcanus was coming, he appointed guards and said to them, "If Hyrcanus comes, do not let him sit down."

When Hyrcanus arrived, they would not let him sit down. He pushed on ahead until he reached the place near Ben Sisi HaKeset. Naqdimon ben Gurion, and Ben Kalba Sabu'a. He sat down among leading citizens in Jerusalem and trembled.

Rabban Yoḥanan ben Zakkai fixed his gaze upon Rabbi Eliezer and said to him, "Deliver the exposition."

"I am unable to speak," Rabbi Eliezer pleaded.

Rabban Yoḥanan pressed him to do it, and the disciples pressed him to do it, so he arose and delivered a discourse upon things which no ear had ever heard before.

As the words came from his mouth, Rabban Yoḥanan ben Zakkai rose to his feet, kissed him upon the head, and exclaimed, "Rabbi Eliezer, master, you have taught me the truth."

Before the time had come to recess the session, Hyrcanus his father rose to his feet and declared, "My masters, I came here only in order to ban my son Eliezer from my possessions. Now all my possessions shall be given to Eliezer my son and all his brothers are herewith disinherited."

A second version is as follows:

His father had many ploughmen who were ploughing arable ground, while he was ploughing a stony plot. He sat down and wept.

His father said to him, "My son why do you weep? Are you perhaps distressed because you plough a stony plot? Now behold you will plough with us in the arable ground."

He sat down and wept. His father said to him, "But why do you weep? Are you perhaps distressed because you plough the arable land?"

He replied to him, "No."

Hyrcanus said to him, "Why do you weep?"

He answered, "I weep only because I desire to learn Torah."

Hyrcanus said to him, "Behold you are twenty-eight years old, yet you want to study Torah? But go, take a wife and have sons, and take *them* to the schoolhouse. . . ."

He arose and went up to Jerusalem, to Rabban Yoḥanan ben Zakkai and sat down and wept.

Yoḥanan said to him, "Why do you weep?"

He answered, "Because I wish to learn Torah."

He said to him, "Whose son are you?" But he did not tell him.

He asked him, "Have you never learned to read the *Shemaʿ* or the Prayer, or the grace after meals?"

He replied to him, "No."

He arose and taught him the three prayers.

Again he sat down and wept.

Yoḥanan said to him, "My son, why do you weep?"

He replied, "Because I desire to learn Torah [and not merely prayers]."

He then taught him two rules every day of the week, and on the Sabbath he repeated them and learned them.

He kept a fast for eight days without tasting anything until the odor of his mouth attracted the attention of Rabban Yoḥanan ben Zakkai, who directed him to withdraw from his presence. He sat down and wept.

Said Yoḥanan to him, "Why do you weep?"

He answered, "Because you made me withdraw from your

presence just as a man makes his fellow withdraw when he has leprosy."

Yoḥanan said to him, "My son, just as the odor of thy mouth has ascended before me, so may the savor of the statutes of the Torah ascend from your mouth to heaven."

He said to him, "My son, whose son are you?"

He replied, "I am the son of Hyrcanus."

Yoḥanan answered, "And are you not the son of one of the great men of the world, and you did not tell me? By your life, today you will eat with me."

Eliezer answered, "I have already eaten with my host."

Yoḥanan asked, "Who is your host?"

He replied, "Joshua ben Ḥananiah and Yosi the priest."

Yoḥanan sent to inquire of his hosts, saying to them, "Did Eliezer eat with you today?"

They answered, "No, moreover, has he not fasted during eight days without tasting any food?"

Joshua and Yosi went and told Yoḥanan, during the last eight days he has not partaken any food. . . .

The sons of Hyrcanus said to their father, "Go up to Jerusalem and ban your son Eliezer from your possessions. . . [As above].

At the banquet Yoḥanan fixed his gaze on Eliezer, saying to him, "Tell us some words of Torah."

Eliezer answered him saying, "Master, I will tell you a parable. To what is the matter likened? To a well which cannot yield more water than the amount which it has drawn (from the earth). Likewise I am unable to speak words of Torah more than I have received from thee." [Note that Yoḥanan actually praised Eliezer as a plastered cistern which loses not a drop.]

Yoḥanan said to him, "I will also tell you a parable. To what is the matter likened? To a fountain which bubbles and sends forth water in greater quantity than it receives. So too, you are able to speak words of Torah more than Moses received at Sinai."

Yoḥanan continued, "Lest you should feel ashamed on my account, behold I will arise and go away from you." Yoḥanan then arose and went outside.

Then Eliezer sat down and expounded. His face shone like the light of the sun and his radiance beamed like that of Moses, so that no one knew whether it was day or night.

He [Yoḥanan] came from behind him, and kissed him on the head, saying, "Happy are you O Abraham, Isaac, and Jacob, that such as this has come forth from your loins! "

Hyrcanus his father said, "To whom does Rabban Yoḥanan ben Zakkai speak thus?"

The people answered, "To Eliezer your son."

He said to them, "He ought not to have spoken in that manner, but thus, 'Happy am I, because he has come forth from my loins.' "

While Rabbi Eliezer was sitting and expounding, his father was standing upon his feet. When he saw his father standing on his feet, he said to him, "My father, be seated, for I cannot speak words of Torah when you are standing on your feet."

Hyrcanus replied to him, "My son, it was not for this reason that I came, but to disinherit thee. . . ."

Eliezer replied, "If I were to seek from the Omnipresent silver and gold, He would have enough to give me, as it is said, *Mine are the silver and gold* (Hag. 2:8) , and if I wanted land, He could give it to me, as it is said, *The earth is the Lord's, and the fulness thereof.* (Ps. 24:1) I sought only that I might find merit in Torah, as it is said, *You spurn all who go astray from your statutes, yea, their cunning is in vain, all the wicked of the earth you count as dross; therefore I love your testimonies, my flesh trembles in fear of you, and I am in awe of your judgments"* (Ps. 119:118) .

Eliezer kept the promises of his youth and became one of the great masters of the next generation. He married the sister of Gamaliel II. A devoted disciple of Yoḥanan, he escaped with him from Jerusalem and accompanied him to Yavneh. After Yoḥanan died, Eliezer left for Lud (Lydda) where he conducted his own court and academy. He was devoted to tradition and conservative in his judicial philosophy. He was finally excommunicated for his stubbornness in holding to ancient traditions and died in retirement after a melancholy old age. When he died, the words of Yoḥanan ben Zakkai lingered on his lips. Three of his sayings were as follows:

"Let the honor of your fellow man be as dear to you as your own.

"Be not easily angered.

"Repent one day before your death.

"Let your honor of your fellow man be as dear to you as your own: how so? This teaches that even as one looks out for his own honor, so should be look out for the honor of his fellow man. And even as no man wishes that his own honor be made light of, so should he wish that the honor of his fellow man shall not be made light of."

Eliezer's disciples asked him, "Does a man then know on what day he will die, that he should know when to repent?"

He replied, "All the more so: let him repent today lest he die on the morrow. Let him repent on the morrow, lest he die the day after, and thus all his days will be spent in repentance."

His unhappy years of excommunication were reflected in the following warning:

Keep warm at the fire of the sages, but beware of their glowing coals lest you be scorched, for their bite is as the bite of the jackal, and their sting as the sting of a scorpion. Moreover, all their words are like coals of fire.

In later years Eliezer's chief rival in the academy at Yavneh was Joshua ben Ḥananiah, Yoḥanan's earlier student at Jerusalem and prefect of his school. Joshua left several sayings as well:

Avarice, an evil impulse, and hatred of mankind put a man out of the world.

What is to be understood by avarice? This teaches that even as a man looks out for his own home, so should he look out for the home of his fellow, and even as no man wishes that his own wife and children be held in ill-repute, so should no man wish that his fellow's wife and children be held in ill repute. There was once a certain man who begrudged his companion his learning, and his life was cut short and he passed away.

The third student, Eleazar ben Arakh, said:

Be diligent in the study of Torah, and know how to answer an unbeliever.

Let not one word of the Torah escape from you.
Know in whose presence you are toiling, and who made the covenant with you.

Eleazar distinguished himself in mystical speculation, which, as we shall see, he learned from Yoḥanan ben Zakkai. After Yoḥanan died, he went to Emmaus, a mountain town which enjoyed a healthy climate, rather than to Yavneh where his fellow students settled. He later lamented:

Settle in a place where the Torah is studied, and do not think that it will seek you, for only your colleagues will help you to hold on to it, and do not rely on your own understanding.

He was a distinguished student who never kept the promise of his youth. He left only one saying:

I am not a prophet nor the son of a prophet, but my teachers have taught me the ancient truth that every counsel enhancing the glory of God leads to good results.

The fourth member of the circle was Yosi the Priest, surnamed "the pious." He said:

Let thy fellow's property be as dear to you as your own, make yourself fit for the study of Torah, for it will not be yours by inheritance, and let all your actions be for the sake of heaven.

Also involved in mystical speculation, he left very few teachings, one of a moral nature. Beluriah the convert asked Rabban Gamaliel:

"It is written in your Torah, *Who shall not show favor* (Deut. 10:17), and it is written *May God show you favor*" (Num. 6:26).
Rabbi Yosi the Priest engaged in a discussion with her. He said to her, "I shall tell you a story. To what is the matter compared? To a man who lent his fellow a coin, and arranged

the time for repayment before the king, and the borrower swore to him by the life of the king. When the time came, he did not repay him. He came to appease the king, and the king replied, 'My claim is forgiven to you, but go and appease your fellow.' Here also, Scripture speaks of sins between man and God, and there, between man and man."

The fifth member of the circle, Simeon ben Natanel, said:

Be prompt in reciting the *Shema‘* and the Prayer [the Silent Devotion]. When you pray, do not make your prayer a matter of routine, but a supplication before the Holy One, blessed be He, for it is said, *For he is a God compassionate and gracious, long-suffering and abundant in mercy, and repentant of the evil* (Joel 2:13). And be not wicked in your own sight.

v. Conclusion

The five disciples of Yohanan ben Zakkai reflected the main concerns of their academy. They sought to find ways to receive the divine words ("Qualify yourself for the study of Torah, since the knowledge of it is not an inheritance of yours."), to apply them to commonplace matters ("Let your friend's honor be as dear to you as your own."), as well as to the broader issues of morality ("Repent one day before your death."), and to abstract from them fundamental principles for the conduct of the good life ("A good heart"). Strikingly, Eliezer, Joshua, and Yosi all repeat the reciprocal rule of good conduct laid down in Leviticus 19:18, "Love your neighbor as yourself," phrasing the law in specific terms (honor, property, reputation). Thus, they tried to bring the word of God to bear on day-to-day issues of life and to create a society capable of accepting and embodying the divine imperative.

It was quite natural that Hillel's teaching that the whole Torah is subsumed under the commandment to love one's neighbor should have dominated Yohanan's circle. Hillel had said, "Go forth and learn." So the students of his disciple went forth and came back with applications of the rule to life. Hillel had also said, "All the rest is commentary." It was this "commentary" that occupied master and disciple. Having met the disciples and considered *their* words, we turn now to the heart of the academy's life: the teachings of the master concerning Scripture.

V. Splendor of Wisdom: The Master

i. The Content of "Torah"

Had a Roman officer, coming up to Jerusalem to help police the vast crowds assembled in the Temple for a pilgrim festival, stumbled upon a small circle of disciples surrounding their master, he would not have thought it unusual. In Alexandria, Antioch, or any of the great cities of the Roman Orient, he would have seen similar groups. What the young men wanted from the master he might well imagine. He himself may have known how, in preparation for a cultic initiation, a neophyte was carefully instructed in the mysteries of a particular salvific cult. He would assume something of the same sort to be happening in Jerusalem. In readying disciples for a rite of initiation or renewal, a master was teaching the mysterious secrets of the Orient.

Seeing the officer, the disciples would hardly have noticed him. What did this curious alien matter to them? Even if he had known their language, would he have understood the words they spoke, words of God and of the mysteries of reality? How inconsequential the disciples would have thought a nation that lacked Torah. The student and the soldier would have understood one another not at all. With the Zealot the centurion could come to terms—upon the battlefield. But why bother with master and disciples? In the world's history they would scarcely register.

For Yoḥanan ben Zakkai, who said man was created in order to study Torah, Scriptural exegesis provided a creative, not merely repetitive or formalized, spiritual experience. The act of biblical study was a religious duty, for, as we have noted,

Scripture and its oral traditions were regarded as the revealed word of the Creator. A generation earlier Hillel had taught that an ignorant man cannot be pious and that the increase of Torah led to the increase of life. A generation later Rabbi Tarfon taught, "If you have studied much Torah, much reward will be given you." A century afterward Rabbi Jacob taught, "If a man is walking by the way and studying, and breaks off to say, 'How lovely is that tree! How fine is that field!'—It is as if he had forfeited his life!" Torah led to wisdom, understanding, good manners, and awe of God. It was the source of virtue in this world and of merit for the world to come. It was held by those who studied it to be a greater honor than priesthood or royalty. Even a sage of illegitimate origin was supposed to take precedence over a high priest who was ignorant of Torah. The study of Torah constituted *the* religious program of the Pharisaic sages.

Although the act of study in the academies produced a social entity and an ethic, the true focus of the sages' concern lay beyond the social consequences of Torah. Benefits for the moral life were only a fortunate byproduct of a deeper and less tangible concern for the word itself. Torah should be studied for its own sake. Reward for study came from the act of study itself, not necessarily from the discoveries of the sage. One certainly ought not to look for base reward. So Rabbi Meir taught in the second century:

> Whoever labors in the Torah for its own sake merits many things, and not only so, but the whole world is indebted to him. He is called friend, beloved, a lover of the Omnipresent, a lover of mankind. It clothes him in meekness and reverence, and prepares him to be righteous and pious, upright and faithful, and keeps him away from sin, and brings him near to virtue. Through it men enjoy counsel and sound knowledge, understanding and strength, as it is said, *Counsel is mine, and sound knowledge, I am understanding, I have strength* (Prov. 8:14). It gives him sovereignty, and dominion, and discerning judgment. To him are the secrets of the Torah revealed. He is made like a self-replenishing river. He becomes

modest, long-suffering, forgiving of insults. And it magnifies him more than all deeds.

In Yohanan's age, Scripture was thought to contain many more levels of meaning than the text yields today. Men discerned a multifaceted Scripture full of hidden messages. The Psalmist said, "Once did God speak, but two things have I heard" (Ps. 62:11). The sages assumed that the Torah was the indivisible, exhaustive account of the event of revelation at Sinai. If at first glance it revealed some truth, careful study would show that it encompassed all truth. The sages' task was to draw out of the given text the widest possible range of insight. Every word was thought to have many modulations of meaning. Each was awaiting the inquiring sage to unfold its special message for a particular moment in time. The Pharisaic sages and Yohanan ben Zakkai among them proposed to draw out that message for their time.

ii. Between Two Revolutions

Yohanan lived between two revolutions in Scriptural interpretation. The first was effected by Hillel. As we have noted, he opened the way to Scriptural interpretation according to the well-known principles of linguistic analogy, inference, association, and deduction. The second came in the generation after Yohanan. The hermeneutic method devised by Nahum of Gimzo and carried forward by 'Aqiba ben Joseph was to expound grammatical parts and other structural elements of the language of Scripture with little or no regard for the actual sense. It neglected the literal meaning of the text. This method, therefore, provided new opportunities to advance textual support in Scriptures for the many kinds of innovation and interpretation that had taken root unnoticed and unintended in the course of generations. According to Nahum and 'Aqiba, every word and letter of Scripture had significance. Even the accusative particle *'et* had to be explained wherever it was found. Some sages were aware of the revolution in hermeneutics which this method implied. Earlier interpretation focused on the meaning, intention, and content of verses, while after 'Aqiba, the form and manner of expression, the very language, and even punctuation were all considered legitimate sources of interpretation. Yoḥanan held ancient traditions and had the capacity to use both Hillel's norms and his own good sense in the interpretation of Scripture. He did not always have the means to discover a scriptural basis for the traditions he held. 'Aqiba, coming after him, found scriptural pretexts for Yoḥanan's traditions.

> That same day [on which Gamaliel II was deposed in favor of Eleazar ben 'Azariah], Rabbi 'Aqiba expounded, *"And every earthen vessel into which any of them falls, whatsoever is in it conveys uncleanness* (Lev. 11:33). It does not say *is unclean* (Qal), but *shall render unclean* (Pi'el), so that it makes other things unclean. This teaches that a loaf suffering second grade uncleanness renders another unclean in the third grade."
>
> Rabbi Joshua said, "Who will take away the dust from off thine eyes, O Rabban Yoḥanan ben Zakkai! You said that another generation would declare the third loaf clean, for there is no verse in the Torah to prove that it is unclean. Now your disciple, 'Aqiba, brings a verse from the Torah to prove that it is unclean! For it is written *Whatsoever is in it shall render unclean."*

Although Yoḥanan read the same Scripture, he lacked the technique to expound it with the philological and grammatical ingenuity of Naḥum and 'Aqiba.

iii. Parables

If in comparison with 'Aqiba, Yoḥanan's use for Scripture was limited, he too used parables and homilies. He carried on theological speculation in biblical terms. He mainly interpreted the literal sense of Scripture. He did not retain, however, the plain meaning of a verse if the obvious sense of the verse appeared incongruous. At times he likewise attached to Scripture a meaning that seemed to him more appropriate and relevant than the plain sense. This is shown in his exposition

of the verse, *Let your garments be always white, and let not
oil be lacking on your head* (Eccles. 9:8) :

> Rabban Yoḥanan ben Zakkai said, "Does Scripture speak
> literally about garments? But how many white garments do the
> pagans have! And if Scripture literally speaks of good oil,
> how much good oil do the pagans have! But Scripture speaks
> only of the performance of the commandments, good deeds,
> and the study of Torah."
>
> Said Rabban Yoḥanan ben Zakkai, "It is like the king who
> invited his servants to the banquet and did not name the exact
> time. The wise among them came and sat at the door of the
> palace, saying, 'Does the king's palace lack for anything?' But
> the fools went about their business saying, 'Was there ever a
> banquet without a set hour?' All of a sudden, the king sum-
> moned them to his presence. The wise ones appeared all dressed
> and cleaned up for the occasion, while the fools appeared in
> their dirt. The king rejoiced to see the wise ones, and was
> angered at the appearance of the fools, and said, 'Those who
> have dressed themselves for the banquet, let them sit and eat
> and drink, while the ones who are unprepared may stand by
> and look at them.' "

White garments were the regular garb of the freeman, and
were especially worn on festivals. Anointing was a sign of
prosperity and Yoḥanan argued that Qohelet (the Preacher)
could not really have meant that the best things in life are
nice clothes or good oil. If that is all that counts, then the
gentiles have a better lot than Israel. This is unthinkable.
Therefore, one must face the precariousness of life by preparing for death and the world to come. Such preparation involved devotion to Torah, commandments, and good deeds.
These represent a trilogy of religious concerns. Torah meant
study of God's word; commandments, the doing of God's
word; and good deeds, the service of the Creator through service of his creatures made in his image. By these three practices
a man might keep himself ready for death:

> Rabbi Eliezer ben Hyrcanus said to his disciples, "Repent
> one day before your death."

They said to him, "And does a man know when he will die, that he should repent?"

He said to them, "Every day a man should say, today I will repent, lest I die tomorrow. Thus all his days will be spent in penitence, and this is the explanation of the matter, *At all times let thy clothes be white.*"

It is instructive to contrast Yoḥanan's use of this parable with that ascribed to Jesus in Matthew 22:1-14 (see also Luke 14: 15-24) :

The kingdom of heaven may be compared to a king who gave a marriage feast for his son, and sent his servants to call those who were invited to the marriage feast, but they would not come . . . .

The king was angry and he sent his troops and destroyed those murderers and burned their city.

Then he said to his servants, "The wedding is ready but those invited were not worthy. Go therefore to the thorough-fares and invite to the marriage feast as many as you find."

And those servants went out into the streets, and gathered all whom they found, both good and bad, so the wedding hall was filled with guests.

But when the king came in to look at the guests, he saw there a man who had no wedding garment, and he said to him, "Friend, how did you get in here without a wedding garment?" And he was speechless.

Then the king said to the attendants, "Bind him hand and foot, and cast him into the outer darkness, there men will weep and gnash their teeth. For many are called, but few are chosen."

The point of the parable ascribed to Jesus is different from that of Yoḥanan's, while the parable itself is quite similar. In the Christian form, the guests refused to attend and others were dragooned, but if they were found unready, they were punished by banishment to "outer darkness." The underlying theology emphasized the requirement of men to be both forever willing and always ready to enter the kingdom of heaven, which was believed to be immediately at hand. By contrast, in Yoḥanan's use of the parable those who prepared themselves for the feast would enjoy it *whenever* it might come. But their preparation entailed not mere *willingness* to attend. It was rather a lifelong *discipline* of preparation through study of the Torah. He believed that the Kingdom of God would indeed come. The great challenge, however, was to prepare for its coming through study and fulfillment of Torah. Yoḥanan thus formulated his program for religion by reading into scriptural phrases categories of religious expression more appropriate, in his mind, than those implied by the plain meaning of Scripture.

iv. Analogical Exegesis

Yoḥanan's attention to the moral appropriateness of Scripture led him to expound its literal sense by analogy to contemporary legal procedure, to past events, or to the common consensus on ethical behavior. The particular form of his analogical exegesis, known as *ḥomer* or pearl, has been compared to the allegorical method of Philo. His known exegeses, however, do not reveal allegorization at all, but rather homiletical moralizing. Others in his time, particularly Gamaliel II and Eleazer of Modin, utilized the same analogical method. It became mostly obsolete when the new hermeneutic of 'Aqiba focused attention on the form of Scripture as much as on its content. By the end of the third century, the method ceased to be employed. The *ḥomer* method was to take the literal sense of Scripture and to suggest analogies to it in legal procedure, past events, or morally appropriate parallels. Thus, Yoḥanan tried to exposit the sense of Scripture in a way familiar to the people of his own generation. We have several examples:

> Five matters did Rabban Yoḥanan ben Zakkai expound in the manner of *ḥomer*.
> On what account did Israel go into exile to Babylon rather than to any other land? Because Abraham's family came from there. To what is the matter comparable? To a woman who was unfaithful to her husband. Where does he send her? Back to her father's house.

Of the first tablets it is said, *And the tablets were the work of God* (Exod. 32:16), but of the second: *The tablets were the work of Moses* (Exod. 34:1). To what is the matter comparable? To a king of flesh and blood who betrothed a woman. *He* brings the scribe, the pen and ink, the parchment, and the witness. If she is disloyal to him, *she* brings everything. It is enough for her if the king will give his signature.

Behold it says, *When a ruler sins, doing unwittingly any one of the things which the Lord God has commanded not to be done . . . he shall bring as his offering a goat . . . it is a sin offering* (Lev. 4:22). Happy is the generation whose prince brings a sin-offering for his unwitting sin!

And it says, *Then his master shall bring him to the door or the doorpost, and his master shall bore his ear through with an awl, and he shall serve him for life* (Exod 2:26). Why was the ear the most fitting of all the limbs? Because it heard on Mount Sinai, *Unto me are the children of Israel slaves, they are my slaves* (Lev. 24:55), and yet the ear broke from itself the yoke of heaven and accepted upon itself the yoke of flesh and blood. Therefore Scripture said, "Let the ear come and be bored, for it has not observed what it heard." Another matter, it did not wish to be subservient to its master, let it come and be subjugated to his children.

And it says, *An altar of stones . . . thou shalt not raise upon them iron.* Now why was iron declared unfit of all metals? Because the sword is made from it. The sword is a means of punishment, and the altar a means of atonement. Keep away that which signifies punishment from that which brings atonement. And behold, just as stones, which neither see nor hear nor speak, on account of their bringing atonement between Israel and their Father in Heaven, Scripture said, *Do not raise upon them iron,* sons of Torah, who themselves are atonement for the world, how much more so none of the destroyers should touch them.

The following paragraph is also presented in the same collection:

And behold it says, *Perfect stones you should build the altar of the Lord your God* (Deut. 27:6). Stones which perfect [the relationship] between Israel and their Father in Heaven, the

Omnipresent said, should be perfect before me. Sons of Torah, who make peace in the world, how much the more so should they be perfect in the sight of the Omnipresent!

Thus the *ḥomer* method was to take the literal sense of Scripture, and to suggest analogies to it in legal procedure, past events, or morally appropriate parallels. Israel was sent back to Babylon as an unfaithful wife is returned to her father's house in disgrace. The second tablets were provided by Moses, as a divorced wife provides the materials for the contract of remarriage. The ruler brings an offering for unwitting sin—would that our rulers were so scrupulous! Would that we had a Jewish ruler! The ear is to be bored as a sign of voluntary slavery because hearing the Torah should prevent it. Iron is not to touch the altar because iron is the material of war. Just as perfect stones (*avanim shelemot*) were used on the altars, so should the sages be perfect in the sight of God. The Torah's penalties are gauged by religious and moral values. Two of the exegeses, the one concerning the ruler (*asher, ashre*) and the other concerning the altar (*shalem, shalom*) are plays on words. These are all, therefore, moral homilies, not allegories in any sense, and are meant to elucidate the commonsense morality of Scripture.

Yoḥanan also commented on the plain meaning of Scripture:

> Woe is us, that Scripture weighs against us light sins as heavy sins. *Then I will draw near to you for judgment. I will be a swift witness against the sorcerers, against the adulterers, against those who swear falsely, against those who oppress the hireling in his wages . . . against those who thrust aside the sojourner* (Mal. 3:5). Woe is us for the day of judgment, woe is us for the day of rebuke! The Scripture juxtaposed those who swear falsely to all the most severe transgressions. Therefore the Holy One, blessed be He, warned us not to swear falsely.

He also elucidated many difficult passages for his students. He thus expounded verses which posed particular difficulty to later critics:

 And out of the ground, the Lord God formed every beast of the field (Gen. 2:19).

 Rabban Yoḥanan ben Zakkai was asked, "Since it is already written (Gen. 1:24), *Let the earth bring forth the living creature,* what is taught by the verse, *And out of the ground the Lord God formed . . . ?*"

 He replied, "The earlier verse refers to creation, while this treats of gathering them together (in order to name them) as you read. *When thou shalt mass (vayyizer-ẓur)* against a city (Deut. 20:19), that is, the Lord God assembled the beasts of the field, which were created from the ground."

He tried also to answer obvious questions that Scripture might pose:

> *And the eyes of both of them were opened* (Gen. 3:7). Then were they blind? Rabbi Yudan in the name of Rabban Yoḥanan ben Zakkai, and Rabbi Berekiah in the name of Rabbi 'Aqiba, explained it by comparing them to a villager who was passing a glass-worker's shop.
>
> Just when a basketful of goblets and cut-glassware was in front of him, he swung his staff around and broke them.
>
> Then the owner arose and seized him, and cried, "I know that I cannot obtain redress from you, but come, and I shall show you how much valuable stuff you have destroyed."
>
> Thus he opened their eyes, and showed them how many generations they had destroyed.

In the course of such homilies, he may have used Scripture to convey his own comments on affairs of the day. Thus, early in his career he taught concerning the verse (Prov. 14:34), *Righteousness exalteth a nation, but the kindness of the peoples, is sin,* that just as the sin-offerings make atonement for Israel, so charity makes atonement for the heathen. After the destruction of Jerusalem, he accepted a strongly xenophobic interpretation of the same verse. His exclamation, "Happy is the generation whose ruler brings an offering on his unwitting sin," may have expressed his distress with the procuratorial government (to say nothing of the Zealots). Likewise, his discussion of the altar as source of peace and not of war would have been especially relevant in the debate on the loyal sacrifices in the summer of A.D. 66, when the question was whether to continue sacrificing in the name of the emperor or not. His counsel of patience at the start of the war also may have found expression in scriptural exegesis.

Through the study of Scripture, men also carried on theological discussion. An issue which troubled the sages was, What is the proper motive from which to serve God? Should man serve him through love ("Thou shalt love the Lord thy God with all thy heart, with all thy soul, and with all thy might," Deut. 4:6), or through fear and awe ("My covenant with him was a covenant of life and peace, and I gave them to him, that he might fear, and he feared me, he stood in awe of my name" (Mal. 2:5). It had been said earlier, "Be not like servants who minister to their master in expectation of receiving a reward, but be like servants who minister to their master in no expectation of receiving a reward." But what motive ought to induce selfless service? In this dispute, Yoḥanan may well have expressed his opinion, not in abstract terms, but in a comment on a scriptural figure. He said that Job had served God on account of fear, as it is written, "The man perfect and upright, and one that feared God and eschewed evil" (Job 1:1, 27:5):

> On that same day [that Rabban Gamaliel II was deposed], Rabbi Joshua ben Hyrcanus expounded, "Job served the Holy One, blessed be He, only from love, as it is written *Though he slay me, yet will I wait for him.* Thus far the matter rests in doubt, whether it means, 'I will wait for him,' or 'I will not wait,' but Scripture says explicitly, *Till I die I will not put away mine integrity from before me,* teaching that he acted from love."
>
> Rabbi Joshua ben Ḥananiah said, "Oh, who will remove the dust from between your eyes, Rabban Yoḥanan ben Zakkai— for all your days you expounded that Job served the Holy One, blessed be He, only from fear, and has not Joshua, your disciple's disciple, now taught us that he acted from love?"

The sages contrasted the service of the patriarchs, which was out of love, with that of the upright gentile, Job, who served out of fear, and praised the "Pharisee for love" over the "Pharisee from fear." Thus Yoḥanan expressed his view that God should be served out of love, by preaching that the upright heathen, Job, served from fear whereas the true motive for a Jew is love.

v. Mystical Exegesis

The study of Scripture reveals something about Yoḥanan's intellectual life. He used Scripture as a means of expressing a wide range of opinion on religious, social, ethical, and political issues. All this represented the outer man, the open and partly recoverable part of Yoḥanan's life. What we know about his inner religious life is contained in stories about his mysticism. We cannot hope to understand much about the mystical doctrines of Yoḥanan's school, for these were kept secret in their own day. The literary remnants, which we shall study, tell us very little about their content. It is Professor Gershom G. Scholem who has uncovered the secret of Jewish Mysticism, especially of that part of Jewish mysticism which was transmitted in the rabbinical academies. (We know little for certain about equivalent Jewish mystical movements outside of the academies.)

The mysticism of the rabbis of the first and second century focused upon a vast cosmic vision of the world. They conceived above the earth seven heavens, beginning with the visible firmament and extending beyond the fixed stars to the highest place, where the Lord himself sat enthroned. If a man were morally and spiritually ready, he could make the ascent to the heavens. There he would achieve communion with God. Two bodies of mystical doctrine existed, which conveyed the secrets of the mystic ascent. One took the form of exegesis of the creation chapters of Genesis; the other, of the chariot vision of Ezekiel. The former centered upon the metaphysical realities of the world. The latter focused upon the configuration of heaven above. The essential task was the contemplation of God's appearance on the throne as described by Ezekiel and reflection about the mysteries of the heavenly throne-world. Scholem stresses what this throne-world meant to the Jewish mystic. It was the focus of his vision of God's throne, which "embodies and exemplifies all forms of creation." All we know for certain about Yoḥanan's mystic doctrine is that it was based upon metaphysical studies of creation and the astral mysteries of the heavenly journey symbolized by Ezekiel's heavenly chariot. Later documents tell us much about how these doctrines developed. Of Yoḥanan's time, all we know for certain is *which* images seemed important to him and what happened when master and disciples talked about these visions. The best we can do in the end is to speculate on what the external imagery meant. The inner quality of the visions we shall never really comprehend. The following is an account of one such vision:

Once Rabban Yoḥanan ben Zakkai was riding on an ass, when going on a journey. Rabbi Eleazar ben Arakh was driving the ass from behind.

Rabbi Eleazar said to him, "Master, teach me a chapter of the work of the chariot."

He answered him, "Have I not taught you thus, *Nor may the work of the chariot be taught in the presence of one, unless he is a sage and understands of his own knowledge*"?

Rabbi Eleazar then said to him, "Master, permit me to say before you something which you have taught me."

He answered, "Say on!"

Forthwith, Rabban Yoḥanan ben Zakkai dismounted from the ass, wrapped himself up in his cloak, and sat upon a stone beneath an olive tree.

Said Rabbi Eleazar to him, "Master, why did you dismount from the ass?"

He answered, "Is it proper that I should ride upon an ass while you are expounding the work of the chariot, and the Divine Presence is with us, and the ministering angels accompany us?"

Forthwith Rabbi Eleazar ben Arakh began his exposition of the work of the chariot. Fire came down from heaven and encompassed all the trees of the field. All the trees began to utter song.

And what was the song they uttered? *Praise the Lord from the earth, you sea monsters and all depths, fire and hail, snow and frost, stormy wind fulfilling his command, mountains and all hills, fruit trees and all cedars* (Ps. 148:79).

An angel then answered from the fire and said, "This is the very work of the chariot."

Thereupon Rabban Yoḥanan ben Zakkai rose and kissed him on his head and said, "Blessed be the Lord, God of Israel, who has given a son to Abraham our father who knows to speculate upon and to investigate and to expound the work of the chariot. There are some who preach well but do not perform well. Others perform well but do not expound well! But you expound well and perform well. Happy are you, O Abraham our father, that Rabbi Eleazar ben Arakh has come forth from your loins."

Now these things were told to Rabbi Joshua while he and Rabbi Yosi the priest were on a journey. They said, "Let us also expound the work of the chariot." So Rabbi Joshua began an exposition.

That day was the summer solstice. Nonetheless the heavens became overcast with clouds. A rainbow appeared in the cloud. Ministering angels assembled and came to listen like people who come to watch the entertainments of bridegroom and bride.

Thereupon Rabbi Yosi the Priest went and told what had happened before Rabban Yoḥanan ben Zakkai.

Yoḥanan said, "Happy are you, and happy is she that bore you. Happy are my eyes that have seen this vision. Moreover, in my dreams you and I were reclining on Mount Sinai when a heavenly echo was sent to us saying, 'Ascend hither, ascend hither! Here are great banqueting chambers and fine dining couches prepared for you. You and your disciples, and your disciples' disciples are designated for the third level of heaven.' "

Other evidence of the transmission of an esoteric doctrine includes the following:

Rabban Yudan bar Pazzi said in the name of Rabbi Yosi bar Yudan: "Three lectured on their Torah before their master, Rabbi Joshua before Rabban Yoḥanan ben Zakkai, R. 'Aqiba before R. Joshua, and before Rabbi Ḥananiah ben Hakinai before Rabbi 'Aqiba. Henceforth their knowledge is impure."

It is taught, Rabban Yoḥanan ben Zakkai said, "What answer did the heavenly voice give to that wicked man (the king of Babylon, Isa. 14:14) when he said, *I will ascend to heaven, above the stars of God. I will set my throne on high, I will sit in the mount of assembly in the far north, I will ascend above the heights of the clouds, I will make myself like the Most High*"?

He continued, "A heavenly voice went forth and said, 'O wicked man son of a wicked man, grandson of Nimrod the wicked who stirred the whole world to rebellion against me by his rule! How many are the years of man? Seventy, for it is said, *The days of our years are three-score years and ten* (Ps. 90:10).

"But the distance from the earth to the firmament is a journey of five hundred years. The thickness of the firmament is a journey of five hundred years.

"Likewise is the distance between one firmament and the other. And above them [the seven heavens] are the holy living creatures. The feet of the living creatures are equal to all of them together, [fifteen, that is, seven heavens and eight interspaces, times five hundred years].

"The legs of the living creatures are equal to all of them. The knees of the living creatures are equal to all of them. The necks of the living creatures are equal to all of them. The heads of the living creatures are equal to all of them. The horns of the living creatures are equal to all of them.

"Above them is the throne of glory. The feet of the throne of glory are equal to all of them. The throne of glory is equal to all of them. The King, the living and eternal God, high and exalted, dwells above them."

"Yet you did say," Yoḥanan concluded, "*I will ascend above the heights of the clouds, I will be like the Most High!* No, but *You shall be brought down to the netherworld, to the uttermost of the pit*" (Isa. 14:15).

Since the content of such esoteric speculation was kept secret in Yoḥanan's day, all one can say with certainty is that there *were* mystical elements in Yoḥanan's thought. Several salient characteristics, however, will suggest what these speculations meant to him. Some kind of ecstatic state certainly was involved though no evidence suggests how it was achieved. Nonetheless, unless the entire account is poetic or fraudulent, the recorded visions of clouds, rainbows, and heavenly fire suggest that Yoḥanan and his disciples saw sights most men do not regularly see. They believed that the sights were real.

The "Babylonian king" had boasted that he would conquer heaven. Once again a pagan king seemed to think that he would "conquer heaven" by destroying Jerusalem's Temple. If Yoḥanan foresaw the destruction of the Temple, the prophecies of Isaiah at the time of Sennacherib were especially relevant to him. He may have been concerned with the prospect that a pagan king would once again aspire to conquer heaven and claim, upon the ruins of the Temple, that he had done so. The boast, *I will ascend to heaven above the stars of God, I will set my throne on high* was a troubling question once more. The answer Yoḥanan gave was to describe the infinity of the distance between man and God, measured by firmaments, living creatures, legs, bellies, necks, and heads. The journey of five hundred times five hundred years conveyed a sense of the majesty and grandeur of the universe beyond which the Creator's throne was stationed. No pagan king could reach such heights. Only a master of Torah could make the ascent.

The mention of the several levels of heaven indicates that Yoḥanan and his disciples were familiar with an earlier tradition, now found in Enoch, II Enoch, the ascension of Isaiah, and a broader rage of mystical speculation. This was also a comprehensible image in the Christian community of Corinth: *I know a man in Christ, fourteen years ago . . . such a one was caught up even to the third heaven, and I know such a man, how that he was caught up into paradise* (II Cor. 12:2-3), Paul wrote. The Corinthian Church, which does not seem to have included many Jews, was expected by the apostle Paul to understand such an experience.

The image of the chariot, so opaque to us after more than twenty-six centuries, had particular appropriateness for Yoḥanan and his disciples. Ezekiel's vision provided a mythical manner of explaining precisely how God had left his sanctuary

before the Chaldean conquest. The Babylonians burned a
burnt Temple. One recalls Josephus' story about the day, before sunset, when chariots were seen in the air and armed bat-
talions hurtling through the clouds, and the holiday when the
priests heard a voice cry, "We are departing hence." Ezekiel
himself had employed this very image to meet the parallel
situation in the sixth century B.C. God, who was believed to
be present in the Temple, abandoned the sanctuary before
the enemy profaned and burned it. So too, the chariot provided a useful means of speculation in the first century. It at
least had special relevance to the impending reenactment of
an ancient disaster. Yohanan not only foresaw the destruction
through scriptural prophecy. Through Scriptures he also offered an explanation of it.

Yohanan blessed his students with a peculiar saying, "Happy
are you . . . who expound well and perform well." It is difficult to understand these words as a one-dimensional reference
to ethical preaching and action. Praise for moral consistency
was hardly relevant in this context. One recalls that Yohanan's
student Hanina ben Dosa had taught, "He whose works exceed
his wisdom, his wisdom shall endure." At face value these
words express praise for one who founds his learning on the
practice of good deeds. But we also remember that Hanina was
a wonder-worker, and "wisdom" had a metaphysical, theosophical, and thaumaturgic dimension. If so, what were these
works? The blessing was for the achievement of a fully realized
gnostic experience. Those who preach the chariot should themselves be able to behold it. Yohanan and his disciples thus
drew upon a continuing tradition of theosophical speculation, using a fund of contemporary, common images as well
as ancient scriptural forms. In moments of ecstasy they con-
fronted the impending disaster in all its metaphysical, mythic,
and theological dimensions.

Some have argued that hidden knowledge was suspect in
Israel's "normative" religious life. Certainly later generations
of sages did neglect Pharisaic mysticism and theosophy. On
the contrary, at this time such visions were crucial to the very
survival of the faith. With disaster impending new questions

were raised, old perplexities renewed. The force of extreme despair swept away shallow certainties. Neither wisdom, wonder-working, nor sacrifice saved Jerusalem. When it was destroyed, some men lost the will to live. Yoḥanan and his disciples endured the disaster and carried on. Some regarded the destruction as the final day in Israel's history and expected the last judgment to take place then. With the Holy of Holies and the city and Temple in flames, they awaited the conclusion of history. Josephus reports:

> They then proceeded to the one remaining portico of the outer court, on which the poor women and children of the populace and a mixed multitude had taken refuge . . . . The soldiers, carried away by rage, set fire to the portico . . . and out of all that multitude, not a soul escaped. They owed their destruction to a false prophet who had on that day proclaimed to the people of the city that God commanded them to go up to the Temple court, there to receive the tokens of their deliverance.

For Yoḥanan ben Zakkai, however, the disaster proved the occasion for regeneration. Having escaped from the city, he and his disciples established at Yavneh a new center for the study, interpretation, and application of the Torah. They affirmed their faith that the Torah remained the will of their unvanquished God. Their duty to obey him endured.

vi. Conclusion

In retrospect, we see that the immediate source of Yoḥanan's courage was the scriptural record of the earlier disaster and reconciliation. Yoḥanan succeeded in renewing the ancient image of prophecy to embody his religious experience. He found in the visions of Ezekiel particularly viable and appropriate forms for his own perception of reality. If our understanding of what these visions meant to him is correct, we discern a very practical consequence of Yoḥanan's dedication to the study of Torah. When Jerusalem lay in ruins, he and his disciples found the faith to continue in the enterprise of the moral intellect.

The study of Torah, which led to ever deeper penetration of the laws of daily life and the mysteries of creation, ought to have disengaged the sages from great historical events. It ever more centered their interest upon the private person. Caught up in visions of the heavens, the sages sought a way of passing from earth through the seven heavens to where the Holy One sat enthroned in his vast and unmeasurable person. The disciples could well turn away from the centurions and the pilgrims round about them. What mattered most was the astral ascent through the heavens to a true vision of the Almighty. This world was a mere vestibule for the next. One could even now take his leave of it, in his senses if not in his body, through the esoteric, celestial visions of which we have here caught only a glimpse.

Here then were the sage's chief concerns: the humble daily life of this world, with its laws and ethical demands, and the metaphysical realities beyond to be reached through mystical experience. The pious man must love his neighbor and cherish his honor, property, and dignity. He must also seek a true perception of the Godhead in all the concrete imagery of the astral mysticism of the day.

Somewhere in between the two worlds of ethics and mysticism, the one commonplace, the other awesome, lay politics and society. Local politics provided few satisfactions. The larger stage of world politics had long ago been closed to Jewish actors. The Pharisees found Jewish society an unpromising arena. Social ties within the Jewish towns and villages were disintegrating. The masses cared little for what the competing sects and parties stood for. Where was a sense of corporateness, of belonging to a larger entity, which would have rendered meaningful a broad social concern? True, most men worshiped at the Temple. But as matters stood, the Temple itself was, to the Pharisees, the least attractive means of achieving social unity and cohesion. And it was unavailable. The sages turned inward, not only because the study of Scripture and its revealed esoteric doctrines and commitment to the private affairs of their own commune were intensely engaging. They turned inward also because they were excluded from world affairs. But they knew they had a better way of dealing with the world, namely through their *own* prayer, study, and mystical and metaphysical experimentation.

Yoḥanan ben Zakkai himself provided the best proof that Pharisees could not hope for worldly success. On the threshhold of old age, he looked back upon a life of partisan dispute, but little real accomplishment. He could not have been more wrong. He who had turned to mystical and metaphysical realities was called by the events of the next fourteen years to take the chief part in this-worldly history. He who had never known success was given the gravest responsibilities of all. In his seventh decade he must have thought himself a soon-to-be-forgotten link in a great chain of tradition. Yet when he died a few years later, he had achieved immortality.

PART THREE: DEATH & REBIRTH
VI. Light of the World

i. Introduction

In April of 66, while Yoḥanan ben Zakkai and his students would have been sitting in the shadow of the Temple mount concentrating on their studies, within the Temple itself and in the city below great crowds assembled. They were listening to another kind of Torah. It was the teaching of zealots and patriots, who shouted angry words at the Roman troops and milled about in the city streets. Eager to act, the people believed their hour had struck. The meager Roman detachments in the city were forced back and mobbed outside the walls. Retreating down the mountain defiles toward their base in Caesarea, the troops were ambushed and wiped out.

Holy war had come. Now the Jews would fight at last. God after all was on their side. Had not their ancestors fought and with God's help overcome foes of greater consequence? Old men in these very streets remembered Jews who knew no ruler but a Jewish high priest. Yoḥanan's own father could have told him of such a day. Among the young men were many whose fathers had said that those had been very good times indeed. Yoḥanan's hours of study were cut short. The Pharisees, who ineffectively had demanded power, were now called upon to join the nation by sending representatives to the revolutionary councils. True enough, the Pharisees did not precipitate matters. Among them, Yoḥanan was probably full of doubts about the enterprise. But the time to act in concert with all Israel had arrived. Where better to begin than in the Holy Temple itself? When more propitiously than during the festival of Israel's freedom, Passover?

Was this truly a "national war of liberation" directed toward bringing the Messiah? Not quite, although at first many thought it was. For much of Palestine, particularly where Jews lived side by side with Greeks, Samaritans, and other non-Jews, the rebellion was seen as mere sedition, a wrongful war. It was quickly suppressed, wherever local Jewish enthusiasts joined in, by Roman troops with the cooperation of local gentiles. Nonetheless, at the outset Palestinian Jewry must in the main have favored the rebels. Most joined in the cheering. Only when they saw the steel of Roman shields and spears glistening in the sun did the morning's enthusiasm evaporate in the noon hour of reality. Then many just went home.

Jewish rebellion actually did overthrow Roman rule in some parts of Palestine, particularly in the vicinity of Jerusalem and in Galilee. The war began as a protest against temporary imperial misgovernment. Once unleashed, however, the emergent discontent within the Jewish population transformed a colonial mutiny into a broad, disorderly, and utopian movement to reconstruct the political and social order. The rebels were hopelessly divided from the beginning. Some of the Sadducees and part of the upper classes in Jerusalem joined in the rebellion. The Pharisaic sect split. Simeon ben Gamaliel led a wing of the party into the revolutionary tribunal. Yoḥanan proposed a pacific policy, although the evidence of his opinions at this time is circumstantial and scant. In any case it is certain that he escaped from the city before it fell in the summer of A.D. 70, probably in the spring of 68, then surrendered to the Romans and was permitted by them to go to Yavneh (Jamnia), a town in the plain where a number of pro-Roman Jewish loyalists had taken refuge.

The rebellion began as a massive riot against maladministration and was led by some of the Temple authorities and reformers within the native aristocracy. The consequent revolution, however, was advanced mainly by two classes, a part of the peasantry, and the urban proletariat, aided by certain fervent messianic nationalists within all classes of the society. In the light of the paramount importance of agriculture, one must regard the decline of small farming, characteristic of large parts of the empire at this period, and the concentration of land in the hands of urban proprietors as fundamental causes of the discontent that led to war. Discontent in Jerusalem, moreover, was intensified by the widespread unemployment caused by the completion of the Herodian Temple, which threw eighteen thousand men out of work. Of the peasant class those in depressed areas most enthusiastically favored war. These were in areas where agriculture was marginal, the back country of Galilee, for example. But in the prosperous agricultural areas, particularly in the Plain, lower Galilee, and Transjordania, the revolution took hold with difficulty, if at all. The larger commercial centers either did not oppose the Romans, like Sepphoris with its mixed population, or surrendered without a fight, like Tiberias. In many of the mixed cities the Jewish population remained at peace. Yoḥanan's later act of surrender must have appeared as neither unique nor treasonable to very large numbers of Jews. If, however, the revolution was fought by economically and socially dispossessed classes, it was led by messianists, ecstatics, patriots and zealots, who formed the revolutionary complex in Jerusalem. The insurrectionary cause benefited from several disparate groups, united by discontent with the status quo for economic, or religious, or political reasons, but divided on everything else.

ii. Counsels of Caution

Yoḥanan had offered his counsels of caution more than two decades earlier. During the reign of Caligula (A.D. 37–41), Jews had destroyed the brick altar erected by pagans at Yavneh (Jamnia). The pagan population had erected such an altar "of the most contemptible materials, having made clay into bricks for the sole purpose of plotting against their fellow citizens." When the Jews saw the altar, they destroyed it and were ordered to replace it. Philo reports:

> So the sojourners immediately went to Capito, who was in reality the contriver of the whole affair; and he . . . wrote to

Caius expounding on the matter, exaggerating it enormously. When he had read the letter, he ordered a colossal statue covered with gold, much more costly and much more magnificent than the rich altar which had been erected in Jania, to be set up by way of insult in the temple of the metropolis.

Petronius, the Syrian legate, was alarmed at the prospect of erecting a colossal statue in the Temple and procrastinated, ordering the Sidonian craftsmen to work with special, painstaking care. Caius' death in the nick of time prevented the orders from being carried out. On this event, Yoḥanan commented: "Do not destroy their altars, so that you do not have to rebuild them with your own hands. Do not destroy those of brick, that they may not say to you, 'Come and build them of stone.'"

Yoḥanan therefore could hardly have favored the irregular actions against native pagan populations, the pillaging of villages, and the slaughter of their pagan populations which marked the onset of the revolution.

A second warning against rebellion may likewise have proven particularly relevant in the spring of 66, although one cannot date it with much certainty. Yoḥanan argued for the observance of biblical regulations on exemption of certain classes from military service. Scripture had commanded (Deut. 20: 5, 8) :

Then the officers shall speak to the people, saying, "What man is there that has built a new house and has not dedicated it? Let him go back to his house, lest he die in the battle and another man dedicate it." . . . And the officers shall speak further to the people, and say, "What man is there that is fearful and fainthearted! Let him go back to his house, lest the heart of his fellows melt as his heart."

On this verse, Yoḥanan commented, in the manner of *ḥomer:*

This law was given in order that the cities of Israel should not be graveyards.
He said, "Come and see how much the Omnipresent pitied

the honor of his creatures. On account of the fainthearted and fearful, when the commander goes through the ranks, he will say, 'Perhaps one has built a house, perhaps another has betrothed a wife, and whoever [so claimed], let him bring witnesses to that effect.' The exception is the fainthearted and fearful. His witness is at hand. He hears the sound of the clashing shields and is frightened, the sound of the neighing horses and trembles, the noise of the horns blasting and is confused, sees the edge of the sword and water runs down between his knees."

Yohanan urged that the revolutionists keep in mind the importance of long-term Jewish settlement in the land and, more important, the abiding dignity of man. War destroyed the work of generations and brutalized those who fought in it. Yohanan held that little could be gained, but much lost, on the battlefield.

Seeing the world as the men of Jerusalem saw it at the beginning of the rebellion, one wonders nonetheless how Yohanan ben Zakkai could have remained aloof from the popular enthusiasm. Rome was suffering its own internal disorders. The eastern empire was turbulent. The revolutionaries hoped that the Jews of the Diaspora, particularly on the other side of the Euphrates, would join them. Throughout this period, Rome and Parthia remained at peace, with Parthia even acknowledging the suzerainty of Nero's government. However, Rome had been preparing an advance into the east and the failure of Nero's plans, mainly on account of the Jewish revolt, had worldwide consequences. When the rebellion began in the spring of 66, the Romans decided that they could not fight on a northern front against Armenia and on a southern front in Judea and diverted troops to the south. The diaspora community in Parthia was not allowed to participate in the rebellion, and there is no evidence that it wanted to; nor was any support whatever received from the diaspora communities in the Hellenistic parts of the Roman Empire. The only exception to the rule of the Diaspora's indifference at this time was Adiabene. But after 70, Diaspora opinion changed on account of the destruction of the Temple. After the death of Nero in 68, the rebellion of the Gauls, Celts, and other peoples augured to some the imminent collapse of Roman hegemony.

Jerusalem, moreover, had strategic advantages. It was well-fortified and enjoyed an excellent water supply. Access to it was difficult. The first successes of the rebels certainly raised hopes of final victory. These hopes, together with economic, social, and political discontent, and the messianic expectations of some circles of Jews, combined to render many men indifferent to counsels of caution. These who shared Yoḥanan's opinion were mainly the upper clergy of the Temple, the members of the upper classes who were responsive to Herodian influence, and a segment of the Pharisees. The groups argued that misgovernment was both temporary and at that time not the private tribulation of the Jews. The maintenance of public order depended on submission to Rome. Thus Ḥanina, the Prefect of the Priests, had said: "Pray for the peace of the ruling power, since, but for fear of it, men would swallow each other up alive."

The subsequent hostility between Jewish parties proved the wisdom of this warning. Later generations accurately commented that Jerusalem was destroyed in 70 on account of "baseless hatred." The insurgents silenced their opponents with their successful siege of the Roman garrison in Jerusalem. They ended the sacrifices offered in behalf of the emperor, thus confronting the country with a *fait accompli*. By the winter of A.D. 66–67, the war had begun. Social revolution was not long in following; the revolutionists burned the palaces and public archives in order to destroy the moneylenders' bonds, to prevent the recovery of debts, and to cause an uprising of the poor against the rich. They established a coalition for revolutionary government. Many loyalists fled the city, and the moderates were brutally silenced.

Yoḥanan ben Zakkai remained in the city for two years, until the spring of A.D. 68. Nothing is known about his actions or opinions in this period. Indeed, one of the conspicuously silent periods of his life is that of the early war years. Talmudic literature does not preserve a single reliable record of his viewpoint on the period between the spring of A.D. 66 and his flight two years later. Yoḥanan had spoken out twenty-five years earlier, to say that destroying altars was unwise since Rome could compel rebuilding them. Some of his statements against forced conscription and in praise of peace ("Whole stones, stone which make peace . . .") *may* date from this period. But they have survived in forms so abstract and indirect that it would be unfair to him to suppose this was all he had to say at such a crucial time. Josephus does not mention him. What, if anything, he said and did his successors did not choose to preserve. What they did hand down were several extremely confused, fanciful accounts of his escape, which are likely to have been based on historical events, but are neither wholly congruous with the events of that period nor internally consistent. All accounts agree, however, that he escaped from the city when escape was still possible, met Vespasian while the city was under siege, prophesied his imminent rise to imperial power, and was permitted by him to go to Yavneh, there to take refuge from the war.

iii. *Vespasian and Jerusalem*

Vespasian had been sent to quell the rebellion and to forestall revolt in the neighboring lands. Bald, rustic, large-jawed, he had grown grey in the imperial service fighting in Germany and elsewhere. He was a sturdy man full of common sense, and his long career had seen numerous good omens. If he believed them, he had sufficient cause to regard his current assignment as highly auspicious. The belief was current that "out of Judea would come rulers of the world." Signs and wonders had long ago pointed to his future distinction. Suetonius, for example, reported:

> An ancient oak tree on the Flavian estate near Rome put a shoot out for each of the three occasions when his mother was brought to bed; and these clearly had a bearing on the child's future. The first slim shoot withered quickly, and the eldest child, a girl, died within the year. The second was long and healthy, promising good luck; but the third seemed more like a tree than a branch.

Later, men saw in both commonplace and uncommon events in Vespasian's long life evidence that he had been destined to become Caesar. A stray dog picked up a human hand at a cross-roads and brought it to Vespasian, "a hand being an emblem of power." A plough ox shook off its yoke and burst into his dining room, falling at his feet and lowering its neck, which was interpreted as a sign of the world's imminent submission. In Greece he dreamed that he and his family would prosper the moment Nero lost a tooth. The next day Nero had a tooth extracted. In Judea when he finally arrived, men fell over one another in their haste to predict his coming enthronement. He consulted a shrine on Mt. Carmel and was promised that he would never be disappointed in what he planned or desired, "no matter how lofty your ambitions." When he captured Josephus, the Jewish general predicted that he would be released from his chains "by the very man who had now put him there, when that man would be emperor."

Further reports of omens came from Rome. Nero had been told in a dream to take the sacred chariot of Jupiter from the temple on the Capitoline to the circus, calling at Vespasian's house as he went. While Galba was on the way to the elections which gave him his second consulship, a statue of Julius Caesar turned of its own accord to face east, and at Betriacum when the battle was about to begin, two eagles fought in full view of both armies, but a third appeared from the rising sun and drove off the victor. While at Alexandria on his way to battle in the Land of Israel, Vespasian had seen many wonders which pointed to him as the object of the gods' partiality. Thus, one of the common people of the city, a blind man, threw himself at Vespasian's knees and implored him with groans to heal him. Tacitus reported:

> This he did by the advice of the god Serapis . . . . Another with a diseased hand . . . prayed that the limb might feel the imprint of a Ceasar's foot . . . and so Vespasian, supposing that all things were possible to his good fortune and that nothing was any longer past belief, with a joyful countenance, amid the intense expectation of the multitude of bystanders,

accomplished what was required. The hand was instantly restored to its use, and the light of day again shone upon the blind.

When Vespasian finally drew near Jerusalem and a Jewish sage named Yoḥanan ben Zakkai greeted him with the words *Vive Imperator,* one thing is perfectly obvious: Vespasian was neither surprised nor displeased. Yoḥanan certainly was not the first such holy man to bring him good news, nor the last.

Vespasian reached Jerusalem after having pacified Galilee, Sharon, and finally the Judean hills. He had moved in no great haste. The situation in Rome was increasingly fluid. The battlefields of the Land of Israel must have seemed far safer than the Roman forum for an ambitious general, especially one who had so often received auguries of coming distinction and had even asked the favor of Apollonius. Vespasian had thus begun his campaign in the spring of 67, a full year after the rebellion and nine months after the subsequent revolution. He had reconquered the lowlands, as the Jewish levies faded before his advancing forces. By the autumn of 67, only Gush Halav (Gischala) and Mount Tabor in Galilee and Gamala in Gaulanitis remained in rebellion in the north. These cities quickly fell during the coming season. For the spring campaign of 68, therefore, there could be only one objective: Jerusalem and final pacification.

Vespasian waited out the winter of 67–68, but the Jews did not. They pursued a vigorous civil war. When the head of the defeated armies of the north, Yoḥanan of Gush Ḥalav (in the Greek accounts, John of Gischala), reached Jerusalem in November of that winter, young and enthusiastic warriors followed him into the teeming city. Reinforcing the extreme elements already in the city and with the help of the Idumeans from the south, they overthrew the coalition regime of Simeon ben Gamaliel and Gorion ben Joseph. In the winter preceding Yoḥanan's escape, the "party of order" lost its hold completely. A reign of terror began in Jerusalem. The former leaders of the revolution now were accused of treason and secret communication with Rome. The new coalition slaughtered Hananiah ben Hananiah, the former high priest, and other nobles and moderates. Yohanan must at this time have determined to escape from the city. Toward the end of the winter, the Roman general staff advised Vespasian to order an immediate general assault. But Vespasian temporized, cautiously preferring to let the Jews fight the Romans' battle against one another. At this time moderates were deserting the city.

The Christian Jews, for example, then fled for their lives. Under the moderate regimes they had no reason to fear the Jewish government. The policy of the Pharisees toward them had always been relatively tolerant. But with the change in government they could hardly hope to continue to enjoy the toleration of Zealot radicals. Hence the conditions of flight which Eusebius reports—an escape under difficult conditions, possibly even under a state of siege, conditions quite similar to those surrounding Yohanan's escape—would probably have prevailed at this time. It would have been especially difficult for an entire community to escape after the summer of 68. At this time, the moderate rebels did begin to desert, as Josephus reports (410–413):

> Of these proceedings, Vespasian was informed by deserters. For although the insurgents guarded all the exits and slew anyone who, for whatever reason, approached them, there were, notwithstanding, some who evaded them, and, fleeing to the Romans, urged the general to protect the city and rescue the remnant of its inhabitants, assuring him that it was owing to their loyalty to the Romans that so many had been slain and the survivors were in peril. Vespasian, who already pitied their misfortunes, broke up his camp with the apparent purpose of taking Jerusalem by siege, but in reality to deliver it from siege.

Vespasian must have had excellent intelligence about what was happening inside the city. After the winter rains in March, 68, he reviewed his armies and sent part of the troops off to clear the rest of the country of rebellion, while he led

detachments against Judea, taking Antipatris, Lud, and Yavneh, finally reaching as far as Emmaus, a mere hour's journey from the city. Only the capital remained. Vespasian went
around it from Emmaus to Jericho and surrounded the city
with camps and garrisons. He needed only to throw up siegeworks. The campaign of spring, 68 ended with the news, received late in June, that Nero had died. Vespasian postponed
his assault on Jerusalem and began the long wait for good
news from Rome. The closest he came to the city, therefore,
was Emmaus at the west and Jericho at the east. Since the
traditions agree that Yoḥanan escaped from a besieged city,
met Vespasian, and predicted his imminent rise to the imperial
throne, we may suppose that this probably happened in the
spring of A.D. 68, sometime between April and June. Before
that time Vespasian was never near Jerusalem, and Yavneh,
Yoḥanan's refuge, was not in his hands until then. After that
time and before the siege of Titus in A.D. 70, escape became
increasingly difficult. Access to the Roman commander required a trip to Caesarea. This spring must have been Yoḥanan's last chance to surrender by escaping through the rebel
lines and into the Roman camp. By every evidence he took it.

iv. The Escape

The sources reveal two traditions concerning Yoḥanan's
escape. According to the first he left the city after the Zealots
refused to surrender to Vespasian, because he was opposed to
the war and hoped to save the Temple. Vespasian had spies in
the city and knew that Yoḥanan favored his cause. When he
came to the Romans, therefore, they recognized him and
brought him directly to Vespasian who received him and
asked what he could do in his behalf. Yoḥanan thereupon
made his famous request for Yavneh, *then* prophesied Vespasian's rise to power. According to a second tradition, Yoḥanan
surrendered, not because he opposed the *war,* but because he
opposed the military *policies* of the Zealots. He favored remaining in the besieged city for a defensive war, rather than
making sorties against the Roman lines. The Romans ac-

cording to this account knew nothing about him, had no special regard for him, and so at his interview with Vespasian he had to justify his actions. Having nothing to his credit, he made a prediction; when it came true, he was granted a small favor.

The classic recension of the first account follows, in Judah Goldin's translation:

Now when Vespasian came to destroy Jerusalem, he said to the inhabitants, "Fools, Why do you seek to destroy this city, and why do you seek to burn the Temple? For what do I ask of you but that you send me one bow or one arrow [as signs of submission] and I shall go away from you?"

They said to him, "Even as we went forth against the first two who were here before you and slew them, so shall we go forth against you and slay you."

When Rabban Yoḥanan ben Zakkai heard this, he sent for the men of Jerusalem and said to them, "My children, why do you destroy this city, and why do you seek to burn the Temple? For what is it that he asks of you? Indeed, he asks nothing of you save one bow or one arrow, and he will go away from you."

They said to him, "Even as we went forth against the two before him and slew them, so shall we go forth against him and slay him."

Vespasian had men stationed inside the walls of Jerusalem. Every word which they overheard they would write down, attach to an arrow, and shoot it over the wall, saying that Rabban Yoḥanan ben Zakkai was one of the emperor's friends.

Now after Rabban Yoḥanan ben Zakkai had spoken to them one day, two, and three days, and they would still not listen to him, he sent for his disciples, Rabbi Eliezer and Rabbi Joshua.

"My sons," he said to them, "arise and take me out of here. Make a coffin for me that I may lie in it."

Rabbi Eliezer took hold of the head of the coffin and Rabbi Joshua took hold of the foot, and they began carrying him as the sun set until they reached the gates of Jerusalem.

"Who is this?" the gatekeepers demanded.

"It is a dead man," they replied. "Do you not know that the dead may not be held overnight in Jerusalem?"

"If it is a dead man," the gatekeepers said to them, "take him out."

So they took him out, and continued carrying him until they reached Vespasian.

They opened the coffin, and Rabban Yoḥanan stood up before him. "Are you Rabban Yoḥanan ben Zakkai?" Vespasian inquired. "Tell me what I may give you."

"I ask nothing of you," Rabban Yoḥanan replied, "save Yavneh, where I might go and teach my disciples and there establish a house of prayer, and perform all the commandments."

"Go," Vespasian said to him.

"By your leave, may I say something to you?"

"Speak," Vespasian said to him.

Said Rabban Yoḥanan to him, "Lo, you are about to be appointed king."

"How do you know this?" Vespasian asked.

Rabban Yoḥanan replied. "This has been handed down to us, that the Temple will not be surrendered to a commoner, but to a king, as is said, *And he shall cut down the thickets of of the forest with iron, and Lebanon shall fall by a mighty one"* (Isa. 10:34).

It was said [this tradition concludes] that no more than a day or two or three passed before messengers reached him from his city announcing that the emperor was dead, and that he had been elected to succeed as king.

This picture of Yoḥanan was evidently drawn from the story of Jeremiah. As the Babylonians had known about Jeremiah through their agents in the city, so Yoḥanan was known to Vespasian. He was received cordially and given the right to reestablish religious life, whereupon he predicted Vespasian's coming election. Josephus reports that he himself reminded the besieged city of Jeremiah's warnings, and one may conclude that Jeremiah's example was not forgotten when later generations considered Yoḥanan's actions at the time of the second destruction. Vespasian's election, however, did not take place for a year after the Judean campaign.

v. Rome and the Pharisees

Yavneh, which had been attacked and burned by Judah Maccabee, had come under Jewish rule at the time of Simon, about 140 B.C., and was incorporated into Jewish territory by Alexander Jannaeus. It was a mixed city with an aggressively anti-Jewish population. During the war Vespasian twice had to establish garrisons in the city. Jewish tradition long regarded Yoḥanan's settlement there as the crucial nexus in the orderly transmission of the authority of the Sanhedrin in Jerusalem to rabbinical courts of later ages. While the rabbinic account is rather fanciful, one must ask whether its essential point is reasonable; namely, Did the Romans *willingly* and *knowingly* permit Yoḥanan ben Zakkai to establish an academy there? I think it likely that they did.

The Romans, first of all, certainly knew that they had an ethnic revolt on their hands. They were anxious not to meet an underground revolution throughout the Diaspora or intervention from Parthia. Therefore, they were careful *not* to transform the war into a religious persecution. Their policy was to divide and conquer. They tried to find allies among the enemy and to discern who could be won over and neutralized. Though they considered the war an ethnic struggle, they did not stop trying to win over all Jews they could reach.

It is clear that they succeeded. First of all, large sections of the Jewish population remained at peace throughout the war. The rebellion in no sense enlisted the support of the entire Jewish population in the Land of Israel. In fact, it progressively lost whatever support it had at the outset. Second, the consequences of the war did not include the destruction of the economy or social foundations of Jewish settlement in the land. The Jewish populations in the mixed cities were molested, but mostly survived the war intact. The Roman policy after the war was certainly not generally to enslave or to deport noncombatant, loyal civilian populations except from the regions in revolt. Most strikingly, there *is* evidence of Roman reconstitution of limited self-government,

if not under Yoḥanan, then surely under Gamaliel II at Yavneh. If the Romans intended to destroy Jewish settlement in
the land, they had sufficient information about what was going
on at Yavneh to know that the activity of the sages there en-
dangered such a policy. They had sufficient force to destroy
that work. They did not do so because they approved it and
hoped to use it for their own purposes.

What, then, was the Roman policy toward the Jews? It
was, first of all, to pacify the country, and this was effected by
military action. More important, the Romans wanted to conciliate Jewish opinion in the vast Diaspora during the war and
in Palestine itself afterwards. That the Romans succeeded in
substantially retaining the loyalty of the Jewish populations
in the Diaspora is proven by the absence throughout the
entire course of the war of significant military or political
support for the revolutionaries on the part of Diaspora communities or from Babylonian Jewry. Indeed, the one instance
of exilic support, that given by the Jewish converts in Adiabene, proves that such support was possible and yet was never
rendered in a meaningful way by the exilic settlements. Josephus wrote his *Jewish War* as a part of the Roman propaganda
effort designed to placate the Diaspora, specifically, the Meso-
potamian settlements, and, as Morton Smith writes, "to demonstrate that the rebels had brought their ruin upon themselves by their own wickedness, that the Romans were not
hostile to Judaism, but had acted in Palestine regretfully, as
agents of divine vengeance, and that therefore submission to
Roman rule was justified by religion as well as common sense."

If this was the purpose of the Roman propaganda, what
then was their postwar policy in the Land of Israel itself? It
was to reconstitute limited self-government among the Jewish
population of the land through loyal and nonseditious agents.
Such a policy would have two favorable consequences. First,
it would further conciliate the Diaspora communities and
demonstrate in action the theory of war guilt advanced by the
Roman propaganda effort. The destruction of the Temple
and enslavement of thousands of Jewish soldiers and civilians
certainly weakened the bonds of loyalty which held the vast

Diaspora communities to the Imperial government. By genuinely constructive and conciliatory actions after the war, the Romans could manifest their true policy: *not* persecution, but tolerance and legal scrupulousness. Second, the survival of the Jewish settlements in the Land of Israel necessitated some form of government. One means which Rome had pursued for almost a century had been through the constitution of native, pro-Roman authorities to continue the type of religious-legal jurisdiction which was so important to the Jews themselves.

Jewish law was obviously going to remain operative among the Jewries of the empire. The Romans made no attempt to stamp out Jewish legal autonomy at this time. If, therefore, they expected to continue it, their best policy would have been, and probably was, to continue its operation through agencies loyal to the government. The situation of the Jews in the Land of Israel made such loyalty imperative since they were close to the Parthian frontier, where additional members of their people lived. It was essential to Rome to regain the sincere loyalty of the Jews, and through loyalists such as Yohanan ben Zakkai they attempted to do so.

That the Romans did so in the manner described by the Talmudic traditions is unlikely. As we have seen, the several reports are neither internally consistent nor congruent with the facts of the imperial succession. Moreover they were written by later generations, who received an account of the events in question after the reconstitution of Jewish self-government had become well established. One may thus regard the story of a smooth transition from Jerusalem to Yavneh with some suspicion. Nonetheless, if in details the several traditions present difficulties, we may legitimately conclude that their point was roughly congruent to the course of events. Yohanan did escape from Jerusalem before its destruction. He did go willingly and with Roman approval to Yavneh. He did begin in an elementary way to reconstitute legitimate Jewish authority there.

Why did the Romans choose the Pharisaic party, which had been one among a number of contending sects before the destruction, to be the instrument of the reconstitution of Jewish autonomy? To be sure, before the war the influence of the Pharisees had been supposedly widespread. If, as Josephus maintains, they favored peace with Rome, their authority had been insufficient to effect that one crucial policy. They were certainly unable to force the priests and Sadducees to conduct the Temple affairs according to their doctrines. Furthermore, at the time of Herod their number was, according to Josephus, not more than six thousand. Faced with the question, Which Jews of those who will work with the government at all can command sufficient popular support to maintain the stability of the Jewish communities in the Land of Israel, the Roman government very likely was guided by three main considerations. First, Josephus wrote his *Antiquities* to provide the answer. As Morton Smith says: "The Pharisees, he says again and again, have by far the greatest influence with the people. Any government which alienates them has trouble. . . . The Sadducees, it is true, have more following among the aristocracy . . . but they have no popular following at all, and even in the old days when they were in power, they were forced by public opinion to follow the Pharisees' orders."

Second, the other parties, as Josephus represents them, were ineligible for serious consideration. The Essenes were "a philosophical curiosity." The Zealots were, as everyone knew, anti-Roman. The Sadducees were an aristocratic minority. Smith comments, "So any Roman government which wants peace in Palestine had better support, and secure the support of, the Pharisees." Thus Josephus himself was probably instrumental in obtaining the recognition of Pharisaic hegemony.

Third, the Pharisees for their part actively advanced their own candidacy as Roman supporters and possibly after Yohanan's death negotiated for it. If so, we discern significant evidence that Yohanan ben Zakkai's policies took hold among the refugee sages at Yavneh. Above any other in his generation, he was responsible for the ultimate success of Pharisaic Judaism, made possible by Roman encouragement and, in unequal measure, by the Pharisaic policy and program. If Rome did recognize the sages of Yavneh as a legally constituted and legitimate authority in the Jewish community in the Land of Israel, we may well regard the accounts of Yohanan's escape from Jerusalem as a legandary, but fundamentally accurate, representation of that recognition.

A final question remains: Why did the Romans burn the Temple? Was it their intention to destroy the Jewish religion? M. P. Charlesworth pointed out: "The only exceptions that Rome made in her general rule of toleration were when a religion appeared to be so closely intertwined with the history and customs of a nation that it fomented or promoted nationalist feeling and led to revolts. After the Jewish rebellion of 66, the Romans destroyed the Temple at Jerusalem deliberately, to cripple the religion." The evidence on the burning of the Temple is equivocal. The Romans through Josephus denied responsibility and attempted to represent it as either an accident of war or the act of the Jews themselves. If the Romans should in fact bear full responsibility, we still must take account of the additional evidence of their postwar policy. So far, I have maintained that Roman policy after 70 by and large did not include the prohibition of the free practice of Judaism, and I think the evidence supports that contention. Assertions to the contrary ignore the events at Yavneh and Rome's willingness to deal with the authority of the rabbinical court as well as her later support for the Palestinian patriarchate. If, therefore, Rome intended to destroy Judaism, she rapidly changed her mind when faced with the realities of the Roman diaspora as well as the Babylonian Jewish community. She indeed may have hoped to destroy Judaism, to be sure, but not so much as to face a massive worldwide and international reaction. In Trajan's invasion of Parthia half a century later, the Romans had to quell just the kind of ethnic revolt they earlier wanted to avoid.

But, destroying the Temple and at the same time disclaiming responsibility constituted a wise and shrewd policy. The inevitable effect of the destruction to the Roman mind may have been the eventual dissolution of Judaism. Without a Temple such as was enjoyed by all other religions, without a cult and a ritual to serve as the focus for the Jews' loyalty throughout the world, the Romans quite naturally expected the Judaism they knew and had to contend with to die out, and with it, in time, the Jewish people as well. Whatever their ulterior motives, however, the Romans made no substantial attempt to outlaw Judaism. Only one religion in antiquity was presistently outlawed and systematically persecuted by Rome, and it was not Judaism, but Christianity. For the rest, sporadic and halfhearted persecutions were occasionally provoked by sedition or war and this, I think, was the case with Judaism, both in the aftermath of August, 70, as well as in consequence of the Bar Kokhba War. By 75, as again by 145, Jewish autonomous government was functioning. That fact is more decisive than the burning of the Temple. Whatever their hopes, the Romans, in fact, behaved in such a way that the destruction of the Temple posed no formidable obstacle to the survival of Judaism. But the kind of Judaism that did survive was different from the predominant forms before 70, and it was a Judaism shaped by men who shared a community of interest with Rome. If Rome wanted to extirpate the Judaism that had caused so much trouble, she enjoyed complete success. What survived in time became a force for peace, not subversion, and its central institutions consistently and, after the Bar Kokhba War, effectively worked to secure loyalty to Rome and tranquillity in Palestine.

vi. Conclusion

Yoḥanan spent the last year and a half of the war isolated from the tragedy at Jerusalem. He must have known that his escape was providential. As the Roman armies pressed closer to the city walls, he saw the fulfillment of his expectation that only a "slight salvation" was possible.

For all the rest of A.D. 68 Vespasian awaited news from Rome. He waited until June of 69, during which time the Roman armies were mostly idle. The Zealots, counterattacking, overran the southern parts of the land. They surprised and took Hebron, a major stronghold. They further recovered territories in Judea which Vespasian had conquered the preceding year. Vespasian had to return in June, 69 to recapture Gophna, Acrabata, and Hebron. By early summer, Rome held the whole country, except for Jerusalem and the fortresses of Herodion, Massada, and Machaerus, south of the city. On July 1, 69, the eastern legions proclaimed Vespasian to be Caesar. He marched to Antioch, thence to Alexandria, and in January of 70 to Rome. Titus carried on the war, advancing on the city with four legions and numerous auxiliary units of confederated kings. In the spring of 70, he began the siege, pressing the lines forward and surrounding the city with a continuous stone wall to cut off escape. The walls were breached in the summer of 70, and the city fell by stages. By September 70, Jerusalem was once again subject to Roman authority. Many were killed and many more sold into slavery until Jewish captives glutted the slave markets and arenas of the Empire. The Temple was burned. Only the Western wall remained. When word reached Yavneh that Jerusalem had fallen, Yoḥanan and his students sat down and wept. The story is told:

> Rabban Yoḥanan ben Zakkai sat and waited trembling, the way Eli had sat and waited, as it is said *Lo, Eli sat upon his seat by the wayside watching, for his heart trembled for the ark of God* (I Sam. 4:13). When Rabban Yoḥanan ben Zakkai heard that Jerusalem was destroyed and the Temple was in flames, he tore his clothing and his disciples tore their clothing, and they wept, crying aloud and mourning.

But even now, with the Temple in ruins, Yoḥanan seemed to remain wholly passive. He had been unable to prevent the war and equally unable to guide its course. His only effective act had been a negative one: to escape the doomed city. Unable to save Jerusalem, he saved himself and his chief students. He was established in benign custody at Yavneh. By the 10th of Av 70, he had given his generation no significant evidence whatever that he was capable of taking responsible and effective action. His discontent in Galilee, his opposition to the priests, his mostly disapproving silence during the early years of rebellion—these now were the public record.

A refugee Jew, happening by Yavneh, would have looked incredulously at the master and his disciples. They were studying just as they had in Jerusalem, talking together as if nothing had happened. True, they wept and tore their clothing. But so did everyone else who heard the disastrous news.

A Roman centurion passing through the vineyard where Yoḥanan was reaching his students would have wondered *who* had made the war, for Jews like those huddled in the shadows obviously had not. If he remembered the same faces in an earlier setting, he would have noted little change. The same serene master sat with the same serious disciples. Once they had studied in the shade of the Temple, now in an arbor. Who is afraid of otherworldly Jews like these? The centurion would have looked for a brief moment, smiled at the thought that here, at least, were no troublemakers, and moved on to weightier concerns. No wonder this weak people would soon pass and be forgotten in history. Hopelessly divided, they could scarcely endure for another century. They fought one another more than they fought Rome. In Yavneh were Jews who ignored the patriot armies and sold liberty in exchange for life. A people relying on such a remnant as this, unconcerned for honor and for liberty, could not long abide. Rome's victory was the final one.

Judea was destroyed, like Carthage long ago. Although, as in Carthage, a few relics still lived on to speak the old language and maintain the old customs, Rome had little reason to concern herself with curiosities. Her rule would last. So let the students pursue their esoteric conversation on antiquities. "Leave them to their idle chatter." His hand on the sheath of his sword, the centurion would have turned away, no more concerned than he had been in Jerusalem a few years earlier. Rome stood eternal.

VII. Happy Are You, O Israel!

i. Introduction

Two roads led out of Jerusalem, one to Yavneh, the other to Masada. Zealots fled to the Dead Sea and barricaded themselves in a massive old fortress of Herod. There they held out for three more years, fighting a hopeless fight rather than surrender. With their wives and children, perhaps a thousand people in all, they withstood advancing siegeworks, engineering marvels, until with the walls breached, they saw at best another day of resistance. That night, the fathers slew their wives and children, and the soldiers one another, until the last Zealot, seeing none alive, slit his own throat. So all was deathly quiet at last.

Rome was surely right, the soldiers must have thought as they entered the smoking ruins of a mighty fortress. She had achieved final victory. Nothing at all remained. The Zealots left no legacy, no vision for the future. They offered no ideal but a military, Spartan one: better suicide than subjugation. If the warriors of Masada represented the only option for the Jews, then and there Judaism would have ended for all time, as the Zealots of Masada supposed it had. The Jewish group may have lingered on, but not for very long.

The road to Yavneh, to the vineyard and the abundant fields and the open port—that was the other way. It was the way taken by the Jews who did not commit suicide and did not regard the disaster as the last drama in a tragic history. They did not suppose that the failure of the sword marked the final catastrophe. These Jews had a better memory of the message of Isaiah, that trust in the sword is arrogance against

God. They kept alive the hope that God, and not the sword, would eventually bring salvation. Yoḥanan ben Zakkai led the way to Yavneh. Because he did, he fathered another generation, and they another. Judaism endured as a living faith and the Jews as an enduring people from that day to this one. Masada and its battlefield bravado was a dead end. Through Yavneh and its tentative, hopeful faith led the way to the future. Masada left behind a few fragments of cloth, some coins, smashed rocks and bones, a monument to futile, barren courage. Yavneh left behind twenty centuries of life, and, I think, many more to come.

But for Yoḥanan the question was, Where to begin? Much was lost, much was even now slipping away. With the Temple gone, who was to give practical decisions which formerly came from the high priests' court? With the city in ruins, what was to become of the great pilgrim festivals? What indeed was to happen to the corpus of law by which the people had lived their lives in former times, now that those who had administered it were no longer able? And what was to be done about the sacred calendar which had been proclaimed in Jerusalem? These were the questions of detail. They presupposed only one thing: the Jews and their ancient tradition would continue to flourish for time to come. But that very conviction met challenge from every side. Few really believed that "Torah" in any form could sustain Israel after so complete a rout of its zealous exponents. Whatever the claims of Yoḥanan and the other Pharisees, it is quite clear that the Torah they exposited and that which the people earlier had wanted to obey and heard from the competing groups were by no means identical. And those whom the people followed to war now had little more to tell them.

The next decade, from 70 to approximately 80, marked Yoḥanan's effective years. Before then, he had sought the power to realize his associates' understanding of God's will for Israel. Now he held that power, but in the most dreadful circumstance imaginable. He wanted to supervise the Temple, not to preside over its ruins. He hoped to direct the lives of Jews toward the will of their Father in heaven, not to mediate between them and their conquerors or to exert authority as a collaborator with the enemy. He sought to convince his Sadducean and other opponents of the rightness of his viewpoint, not to inherit their wreckage in the hour of universal disaster. And above all, he intended to instruct his students in the right path, not to send them forth as agents of a foreign army of occupation. So the irony of Yohanan's life must now have yielded bitter reflection, for he had gotten just what he wanted, but not in the way he had envisaged.

What indeed were his alternatives at Yavneh? He could have chosen to live as before, master of a circle of disciples, leader of one party in a bitterly divided population. If others had taken up the daily task, perhaps Yohanan would have chosen such a life. Passing his seventieth year, where was he to find the energy and vigor for another active career? He could, alternatively, have addressed to the people one final bitter sermon: "You were forewarned, and now bear the disagreeable consequence of your indifference." And he could thereupon have turned his back upon the country and its leaderless, heartbroken masses. How tempting it must have been to say to the world, "I who share your fate bid you a last farewell," and to retire to some foreign exile or to a barren wilderness, there to start a commune, the "new Israel" of the future. Scripture prevented it. Moses, tempted to create of his own seed a new Israel, reminded God that all he had, and all he ever would have, was the old one. Jeremiah, weeping for the destruction of his people, purchased land to signify that once again in the Land of Israel would be heard the voice of rejoicing and of laughter, the voice of the bridegroom and the bride. He chose to stay at home and to bind up the broken spirit of the remnant left behind.

How could Yohanan ben Zakkai do otherwise than give his last, best years to the surviving Jews and their government? Now he must have understood the ultimate meaning of the years of preparation, deep isolation and then conflict, and rigorous study. The Galilee he left behind so long ago had now become the country's chief resource. If it hated the sages' Torah, today it needed the instruction which only expositors of Torah such as Yoḥanan could offer. Jerusalem, so long ago destined for destruction, now lay in ruins. Nothing was left to purify. Only Torah could speak for her. "Forty years in business, forty years in study"—and now? He knew he had little time. Even of that, the tired old man could hardly be certain. Jeremiah was left a few years, perhaps five at most, and achieved nothing after the destruction of the First Temple. Perhaps, however he might will it, Yoḥanan could not carry through the task he now dreamed of doing. We today know otherwise, but then how could he have been sure? With hindsight, we doubt that Yoḥanan could have done other than take up the duties of a dreadful hour. He would in a few critical years insure the continued prosperity of the ancient tradition in the *very* form he gave to it. But faced with the same grave crisis, others may not have had the audacity to try.

Here we perceive another unexpected consequence of the years of fruitless strife. Yoḥanan was not used to success and was therefore quite prepared to struggle tenaciously without its slightest prospect. Eighteen years in the Galilee produced little result, but he stayed there all those eighteen years. A lesser man would have gone away after one or two. Twenty-five years in Jerusalem left him an exhausted old man, without much influence over public opinion and with practically none at all at the Temple. And still he struggled that quarter of a century. The years hardened him and taught him to accept defeat and to fight again. He now no longer had even to expect success in order to justify the effort. He needed only to think the effort necessary, whatever the outcome. Even when he died, he did not claim he had done much to merit great reward. He prevailed, not only against what seemed inexorable history, but against the natural inclinations of the heart. So too Jeremiah, who knew his own frailty and perceived the heart's inconstancy, nonetheless spoke the words that burned within him, while almost certain he would be repaid by assassination. But to Jeremiah came the reassuring word of God. Yoḥanan depended only upon faith, the echo of that word in Scripture and tradition.

ii. Theological Challenge

We understand why Yoḥanan ben Zakkai must have turned, first of all, to the problem of faith. At Yavneh his attention was drawn to the deep despair of the Jews. With Jerusalem in Roman hands and the Temple in ruins, some saw themselves as the rejected children of God, born to disaster. Others accepted the prophetic teaching that suffering was punishment for sin and reflected more thoughtfully on the nature of human transgression. They reconsidered ancient analyses of man's shortcoming in the light of the fresh catastrophe. Still others, both on the Roman and the Jewish sides as well as within the nascent Christian community, offered an explanation of the cataclysm in terms of their own understanding of human history. Most were obsessed with the recent unfortunate events. They wondered what to make of the national disaster. The result was preoccupation with the future and hope for quick recompense.

Yoḥanan differed from the rest of his generation. He concerned himself with the prevailing needs of the surviving remnant of Israel. While he shared the common sense of tragedy and endured the despair of his generation, he did not fix his vision on what had happened and what would come to compensate for the catastrophe. He, instead, attempted to devise a program for the survival and reconstruction of the Jewish people and faith. Thus, retrospectively, a paradox emerges. Out of preoccupation with the sufferings of the past came neurotic obsession with the secret of future redemption. From stubborn consideration of present and immediate difficulties came a healthy, practical plan by which Israel might in truth hold on to what could be saved from the disaster. Others offered the comfort that as certainly as punishment has followed sin, so surely would he who chastised the people comfort, then redeem them. Therefore Israel ought to wait for inexorable redemption. Yoḥanan, on the other hand, proposed a program and a policy for the interim during which the people had to wait.

The people had to be told, first of all, why they suffered.

Romans and Jewish loyalists, Jewish-Christians, Jewish apocalyptics, and Yoḥanan—all advanced answers to this question,
agreeing that the sin of Israel had brought disaster, but dis-
agreeing on precisely what that sin was. The obvious answer,
given by the victorious party, was that Israel had sinned by relying on force of arms, by rebelling against Roman rule.
Josephus in the *War* emphasized that the sins of the nation
had guaranteed the Roman victory: "Invariably arms have
been refused to our nation, and warfare has been the sure
signal of defeat. For it is, I suppose, the duty of the occupants
of holy ground to leave everything to the rule of God, and
to scorn the aid of human hands, can they but conciliate the
Arbiter above." Josephus was particularly concerned about
driving home this point, because the Romans had hired him
to write the book partly in order to dissuade the Jews of Mesopotamia and Babylonia from trying to secure Parthian intervention in Palestine. The Romans likewise regarded the catastrophe as direct recompense for rebellion against Rome, a sin
compounded by the sheer inconvenience of the war, coming
when the imperial succession was in doubt, other lands in
revolt, and the armies fighting a civil war. Josephus reported
Titus thus addressed the city:

> You without bestowing a thought on our strength or your
> own weakness have through inconsiderate fury and madness
> lost your people, your city, and your Temple.
> You were incited against the Romans by Roman humanity.
> . . . We allowed you to occupy this land, and set over you
> kings of your own blood; then we maintained the laws of your
> forefathers, and permitted you . . . to live as you willed.

Nonetheless, Israel had rebelled. Whose fault was it then that
the Temple was destroyed? Israel sinned by the act of war and
was punished by conquest. In later decades even some Jews
came to see matters in this way, but only after the utter de-
vastation of vast territories in the Bar Kokhba rebellion sixty-
five years later.

The Christian Jews of Jerusalem had held the Temple
sacred for thirty years, participating in its rites and frequent-

ing its courts. After the destruction, the Christian community held that the final punishment had at last come on the people who had rejected Jesus Christ. The Church naturally came to regard the catastrophe as a vindication of Christian faith. Eusebius preserved the Christian viewpoint:

> Those who believed on Christ migrated from Jerusalem, so when holy men had altogether deserted the royal capital of the Jews . . . the judgment of God might at last overtake them for all their crimes against Christ and his apostles, and all that generation of the wicked be utterly blotted out from among men. . . . Such was the reward of the iniquity of the Jews and of their impiety against the Christ of God.

The Christians thus thought that Jerusalem had suffered the punishment of its inhabitants, who had sinned against Christ.

The Jewish apocalyptics likewise blamed Israel's sins for the disaster, meditated on the nature of sin, and comforted the people with the promise of impending redemption, of which they declared, "Thrice blest the man who lives until that time." Two documents, the apocalypse of Ezra and the vision of Baruch, are representative of the apocalyptic state of mind. The author (or editor) of the Ezra apocalypse (II Ezra 3-14), who lived at the end of the first century A.D., looked forward to a day of judgment when the Messiah would destroy Roman power, and the rule of God would govern society. He wondered at the same time how Israel's continued sufferings might be reconciled with divine justice. To Israel, God's will had been revealed, but God had not removed the evil inclination which prevented the people from carrying out that will: "For we and our fathers have passed our lives in ways that bring death. . . . But what is man, that thou art angry with him, or what is a corruptible race, that thou art so bitter against it?" (Ezra 8:26) Ezra was told that God's ways are inscrutable (4:10-11), but when he repeated the question, "Why has Israel been given over to the gentiles as a reproach," he was given an answer characteristic of this literature. A new age is dawning which will shed light on such perplexities. Thus he was told:

162

If you are alive, you will see, and if you live long, you will often marvel, because the age is hastening swiftly to its end. For it will not be able to bring the things that have been promised to the righteous in their appointed times, because this age is full of sadness and infirmities (4:20-26).

An angel told him the signs of the coming redemption, saying:

The sun shall suddenly shine forth at night and the moon during the day, blood shall drip from wood, and the stone shall utter its voice, the peoples shall be troubled, and the stars shall fall (5:4-5).

And he was admonished to wait patiently:

The righteous therefore can endure difficult circumstances, while hoping for easier ones, but those who have done wickedly have suffered the difficult circumstances, and will *not* see easier ones (6:55-56).

The pseudepigraphic Ezra thus regarded the catastrophe as the fruit of sin, more specifically, the result of man's *natural* incapacity to do the will of God. He prayed for forgiveness and found hope in the coming transformation of the age and the promise of a new day, when man's heart will be as able, as his mind even then was willing, to do the will of God.

The pseudepigraph in the name of Jeremiah's secretary, Baruch, likewise brought promise of coming redemption, but with little practical advice for the intervening period. The document exhibited three major themes. First, God acted righteously in bringing about the punishment of Israel:

Righteousness belongs to the Lord our God, but confusion of face to us and our fathers. . . . The Lord has brought them upon us, for the Lord is righteous in all his works (Baruch 2:6).

Second, the catastrophe came on account of Israel's sin:

Why is it, O Israel . . . that you are in the land of your enemies? . . . You have forsaken the fountain of wisdom, if you had walked in the way of the Lord, you would be dwelling in peace forever (3:10).

Third, as surely as God had punished the people, so certainly would he bring the people home to their land and restore their fortunes. Thus Jerusalem speaks:

> But I, how can I help you? For He who brought these calamities upon you will deliver you from the hand of your enemies. . . . Take courage, my children, cry to God, and He will deliver you from the power and hand of the enemy. . . . For I sent you out with sorrow and weeping, but God will give you back to me with joy and gladness forever (4:17-18, 21, 23).

Finally, Baruch advised the people to wait patiently for redemption, saying:

> My children, endure with patience the wrath that has come upon you from God. Your enemy has overtaken you, but you will soon see their destruction and will tread upon their necks. . . . Take courage, my children, and cry to God, for you will be remembered by Him who brought this upon you. For just as you purposed to go astray from God, return with tenfold zeal to seek Him, for He who brought these calamities upon you will bring you everlasting joy with your salvation. Take courage, O Jerusalem, for He who named you will comfort you (4:25, 27-30).

This theme came very close to Yoḥanan's comments on the destruction, for Baruch emphasized, as did Yoḥanan, the comfort to be found in the very authorship of the calamity. Yoḥanan however emphasized the duty of the people to repent and return to God as the *condition* of redemption. Baruch regarded redemption as a present hope, which would be fulfilled in a short while, while Yoḥanan gave no indication except in his very last breath that he expected the redemption in the near future. So far as the consolation of Baruch depended on immediate redemption, it thus was not consonant with the opinions of Yoḥanan ben Zakkai, who never said, "Endure with patience . . . because redemption is close at hand."

iii. Yoḥanan's Response

Yoḥanan, always skeptical of messianic movements among the people, taught:

If you have a sapling in your hand, and it is said to you, 'Behold, there is the Messiah'—go on with your planting, and afterward go out and receive him. And if the youths say to you, 'Let us go up and build the Temple,' do not listen to them. But if the elders say to you, 'Come, let us destroy the Temple,' listen to them. The building of youth is destruction, and the destruction of old age is building—proof of the matter is Rehoboam, son of Solomon.

Yoḥanan offered not hope of speedy redemption, but rather a conditional promise: just as punishment surely followed sin, so will redemption certainly follow *repentance*.

Yoḥanan was not immune to the widespread sense of despair, for he changed his interpretation of the verse, "Righteousness exalts a nation, but the kindness of the peoples is sin (Prov. 14:34). Earlier he had taught that just as a sin-offering makes atonement for Israel, so does loving-kindness make atonement for the heathen. But after the destruction, he accepted an xenophobic interpretation:

Rabban Yoḥanan ben Zakkai said to his disciples, "My sons, what is the meaning of the verse, *Righteousness exalts a nation, and the kindness of the peoples is sin* (Prov. 14:35) "?

Rabbi Eliezer answered and said, "*Righteousness exalts a nation*—this refers to Israel, of whom it is said, *Who is like Your people Israel, one nation in the earth* (II Sam. 7:23). *And the kindness of the peoples is sin*—the good deeds are a sin to the nations of the world, for they do them only to make themselves great, as it says, *That they may offer sacrifices of sweet savor unto the God of Heaven, and pray for the life of the king and of his sons* (Ezra 6:10) ."

Rabbi Joshua answered and said, "*Righteousness exalts a nation*—this refers to Israel, of whom it is written, *Who is like Your people Israel, one nation in the earth? And the kindness of peoples is sin*—all the kindness and charity that

165

the heathen do is regarded as a sin because they only do it to prolong their dominion, as it written, *Wherefore, O King let my counsel be acceptable to You, and break off your sins by righteousness and your iniquities by showing mercy to the poor, that there may be a lengthening of thy tranquillity* (Daniel 4:27) ."

Rabbi Eleazar ben Arakh answered and said, "*Righteousness exalts a nation,* and [so does] kindness—this is Israel, but to the nations of the world [belongs] sin."

Rabban Yoḥanan ben Zakkai said, "I prefer the words of Rabbi Eleazar ben Arakh to my and your words, for he assigns righteousness and kindness to Israel, and sin to the nations of the world."

This shows that he also had given an answer. What had it been? As it has been taught: Rabban Yoḥanan ben Zakkai had earlier said to them, "Just as the sin-offering makes atonement for Israel, so charity makes atonement for the heathen."

Yoḥanan had a detailed, practical program to offer for the repair of the Jewish soul and reconstruction of the social and political life of the Land of Israel. It was, first, to provide the people with a source of genuine comfort by showing them how they might extricate themselves from the consequences of their sins. Second, he placed new emphasis upon those means of serving the Creator which had survived the devastated sanctuary. Finally, he offered a comprehensive program for the religious life, a program capable of meeting this and any future vicissitude in Israel's history. By concentrating on the immediate problems of the day, Yoḥanan showed how to transcend history itself—not through eschatological vision, but through concrete actions in the workaday world. His message of comfort was preserved in this story:

> *Because thou didst not serve the Lord thy God with joyfulness and gladness of heart, by reason of the abundance of all things, therefore thou shalt serve thine enemies whom the Lord will send against thee in hunger and thirst, in nakedness and in want of all things* (Deut. 28:47) .

Once Rabban Yoḥanan ben Zakkai was going up to Emmaus

in Judea, and he saw a girl who was picking barley-corn out of the excrement of a horse.

Said Rabban Yoḥanan ben Zakkai to his disciples, "What is this girl?"

They said to him, "She is a Jewish girl."

"And to whom does the horse belong?"

"To an Arabian horseman," the disciples answered him.

Then said Rabban Yoḥanan ben Zakkai to his disciples, "All my life I have been reading the following verse, and I have not until now realized its full meaning: *If you will not know, O fairest among women, follow in the tracks of the flock, and pasture your kids beside the shepherds' tents* (Song of Songs 1:8).

"You were unwilling to be subject to God, behold now you are subjected to the most inferior of nations, the Arabs. You were unwilling to pay the head-tax to God, *a beqa a head* (Exod. 38:26). Now you are paying a head-tax of fifteen sheqels under a government of your enemies.

"You were unwilling to repair the roads and streets leading up to the Temple. Now you have to keep in repair the posts and stations on the road to the imperial cities. And thus it says, *Because thou didst not serve. . . . .* Because you did not serve the Lord your God with love, therefore you shall serve your enemy with hatred. Because you did not serve the Lord your God when you had plenty, therefore you shall serve your enemy in hunger and thirst. Because you did not serve the Lord your God when you were well clothed, therefore you shall serve your enemy in nakedness. Because you did not serve the Lord your God by reason of the abundance of all things, therefore shall you serve your enemy in want of all things."

Yoḥanan thereupon exclaimed, "Happy are you, O Israel! When you obey the will of God, then no nation or race can rule over you! But when you do not obey the will of God, you are handed over into the hands of every low-born people, and not only into the hands of the people but even into the power of the cattle of that low-born people."

This incident epitomizes Yoḥanan's viewpoint on the disaster. He never said, "Take comfort because in a little while, suffering will cease." Yoḥanan called on the people to *achieve* a better fortune through their own efforts. Like Josephus, he taught that Israel can be happy if she submits to God and to the Romans and follows the laws laid down by both. Both conceived of the fulfillment of Jewish law as interpreted by the Pharisees to be the good life in this world and assurance of a portion in the next. Yohanan, unlike Josephus, did not go to Rome, but remained at home among the suffering folk.

In later years Rabbi 'Aqiba, believing that Ben Koziba (Bar Kokhba) was the Messiah, became impatient with the results of Yohanan's limited program. He urged his followers to rebel once again. This act represented the failure of courage, the nerve to wait. Because the people had grown impatient with their own capacities, they looked to God for immediate deliverance. The consequence was a new revolution. Another rabbi rebuked 'Aqiba: "Grass will grow on your cheeks, 'Aqiba ben Joseph, but the Messiah will not have appeared." In the meantime, however, the nation was plunged once again into revolution and met a far greater disaster than before.

iv. "For I Desire Mercy, Not Sacrifice"

Yohanan had earlier taught, in commenting on the words of Qohelet, "Let your garments always be white, and let not oil be lacking on your head" (Eccles. 9:8), that Jews should clothe themselves in Torah, commandments, and acts of kindness. Each of these categories represented a fundamental concern of the pious man. Through the study of Torah man learned what the God wanted of him. Through doing the commandments, he carried out that will. Through acts of loving-kindness he freely honored God who gave the Torah. These elements were probably a transformation of the teachings of Simeon the Righteous two centuries earlier: "On three things does the age stand: on the Torah, on the Temple service, and on acts of piety." By "Torah" Simeon had meant the books of the Torah; by "Temple service," the sacrificial cult in Jerusalem; by "acts of piety," acts of loyalty and obedience to God. Yohanan survived the destruction of the Temple. He came at the end of a long struggle for the Torah, both written and oral, as interpreted by the Pharisees. Acts of obedience to God seemed to him to comprehend a broader obligation than piety. He therefore infused these categories with new content. We here see his thought:

> Once as Rabban Yohanan ben Zakkai was coming out of Jerusalem, Rabbi Joshua followed him, and beheld the Temple in ruins.
> "Woe unto us," Rabbi Joshua cried, "that this place, the place where the iniquities of Israel were atoned for, is laid waste."
> "My son," Rabban Yohanan said to him, "be not grieved. We have another atonement as effective as this. And what is it? It is acts of lovingkindness, as it is said, *For I desire mercy, not sacrifice* (Hos. 6:6) ."

Yohanan's treatment of the verse, "For I desire mercy, not sacrifice," was consistent with the contemporary hermeneutic. In biblical times, *hesed* had meant (in part) the mutual liability of those who are friends and relatives, master and servant, or any relationship of joint responsibility. In relationship to God *hesed* meant acts of conformity to the covenant between man and God. Hosea meant that God demanded loyal adherence to his covenant, rather than sacrifice. By Yohanan's time, however, the word had acquired a different connotation. It meant mercy or an act of compassion and lovingkindness. Thus to Jesus of Nazareth was attributed the saying: "Those who are well have no need of a physician, but those who are sick. Go and learn what this means, 'I desire mercy [eleon] and not sacrifice.' For I came not to call the righteous, but sinners" (Matt. 9:12-13) . Later rabbinic sources likewise preserved this connotation in commenting on the verse. The verse was likewise understood in the *Recognitions of Clement,* in an exegesis strikingly similar to Yohanan's:

> This place which seemed chosen for a time, often harassed as it had been by hostile invasions and plunderings, was at last to be wholly destroyed. And in order to impress this upon them even before the coming of the true prophet, who was

to reject at once the sacrifices and the place, it was often plundered by enemies and burnt with fire, and the people carried into captivity among foreign nations, and then brought back when they betook themselves to the mercy of God; that by these things they might be taught that a people who offer sacrifices are driven away and delivered up into the hands of the enemy, but they who do mercy and righteousness are without sacrifices freed from captivity and restored to their native land.

Yohanan thought that through *hesed* the Jews might make atonement, and that the sacrifices now demanded of them were love and mercy. His choice of the verse in Hosea gave stress to the ethical element of his earlier trilogy of the study of Torah, doing the commandments, and acts of loving-kindness. Yohanan emphasized the primacy of *hesed* itself in the redemptive process: *Just as the Jews needed a redemptive act of compassion from God, so must they now act compassionately in order to make themselves worthy of it.* This primary emphasis in personal moral quality rather than specific external action, either ritual or legal, is in accordance with the increasing concern for the inner aspect of religion characteristic of the age. The act of compassionate fellowship, which in Yohanan's opinion was the foundation of true religion, became the central focus of his consoling message for the new and troubled age.

Yohanan shared the common sense of grief and taught, like others, that the sins of the nation had brought the disaster. But he added, its virtues might bring redemption. He differed from others in rejecting the eschatological focus of consolation. He offered the ideal of *hesed,* a means by which Jews might change their own hearts. He provided an interim ethic by which the people might live while they awaited the coming redemption. The earlier age had stood on the books of the Torah, the Temple rites, and acts of piety. The new age would endure on the foundation of studying the Torah, doing the commandments, and especially performing acts of compassion. Compassion strikingly embodied that very quality which the brutality of war must paradoxically have accen-

tuated in his mind: man's capacity to act kindly and decently
to his fellow man.

The consequence of Yoḥanan's lesson may have been embodied in a later encounter between his disciple Joshua and a
group of apocalyptists. One recalls that II Baruch had lamented:

Blessed is he who was not born, or he who having been born
has died,

But as for us who live, woe unto us. Because we see the afflictions
of Zion, and what has befallen Jerusalem. . . .

You husbandmen, sow not again.

And earth, why do you give your harvest fruits?

Keep within yourself the sweets of your sustenance.

And you, vine, why do you continue to give your wine?

For an offering will not again be made therefrom in Zion,

Nor will first-fruits again be offered.

And do you, O heavens, withhold your dew,

And open not the treasuries of rain.

And do you, sun, withhold the light of your rays,

And you moon, extinguish the multitude of your light.

For why should light rise again

Where the light of Zion is darkened?

Would that you had ears, O earth,

And that you had a heart, O dust,

That you might go and announce in Sheol,

And say to the dead,

"Blessed are you more than we who live."

(II Baruch, 10:6-7, 9-12; 11:6-7)

Yoḥanan's student Joshua met such people. It was reported
that when the Temple was destroyed, ascetics multiplied in
Israel, who would not eat flesh or drink wine. Rabbi Joshua
dealt with them:

He said to them, "My children, On what account do you not
eat flesh and drink wine?"

They said to him, "Shall we eat meat, from which they used
to offer a sacrifice on the altar, and now it is no more? And

shall we drink wine, which was poured out on the altar, and now it is no more?"

He said to them, "If so, we ought not to eat bread, for there are no meal offerings any more. Perhaps we ought not to drink water, for the water-offerings are not brought anymore."

They were silent.

He said to them, "My children, come and I shall teach you. Not to mourn at all is impossible, for the evil decree has already come upon us. But to mourn too much is also impossible, for one may not promulgate a decree for the community unless most of the community can endure it. . . . But thus have the sages taught: 'A man plasters his house, but leaves a little piece untouched. A man prepares all the needs of the meal, but leaves out some morsel. A woman prepares all her cosmetics, but leaves off some small item.' "

v. Conclusion

I do not believe that Yoḥanan's words to Joshua—"My son, be not grieved; we have another atonement as effective as this. And what is it? It is acts of loving-kindness, as it is said, 'For I desire mercy, not sacrifice' (Hos. 6:6) "—have been more penetratingly elucidated than by Judah Goldin:

This anecdote . . . reports a revolutionary discovery . . . that, unlike what all the historic religions display, unlike even the natural impulse of every pious creature to bring something to, do something for, his God—as any lover is frustrated if he is reduced to words only—it *is* possible to worship God and to show one's love for and to Him, without giving Him a material gift. In at least this respect He is unique. If we cannot win His good opinion by means of holocausts, we can win it by acts of lovingkindness to our fellowman. An idea like this takes a long time to sink in, and in reality it never entirely displaces the primary impulse. If only there were the Temple: what a busyness could go on, what a tangible reassurance it would be to see the High Priest change from one set of garments to another.

The change spoken of here took place not formally, but in the heart. What Yoḥanan demanded was that Israel now see, in its humble day-to-day conduct, deeds of so grand a dimension as to rival the sacred actions, rites, and gestures of the Temple.

If we appreciate the force of powerful emotions aroused by the Temple cult, we may understand how grand a revolution was effected in the simple declaration, so long in coming, that with the destruction of the Temple the realm of the sacred had finally overspread the world. Man must now see in himself, in his selfish motives to be immolated, the noblest sacrifice of all. So Rabban Gamaliel son of Rabbi Judah the Patriarch said, "Do His will as if it was your will, so that He may do your will as if it was His will. Make your will of no effect before His will, that He may make the will of others of no effect before your will." His will is that men love their neighbors as themselves. Just as willingly as men would contribute bricks and mortar for the building of a sanctuary, so willingly ought they to contribute love, renunciation, self-sacrifice, for the building of a sacred community. If one wants to do something for God in a time when the Temple is no more, the offering must be the gift of selfless compassion. The holy altar must be the streets and marketplaces of the world.

Yoḥanan ben Zakkai thus accomplished more than he had set out to do. He began to restore the broken heart of a nation. In the end he accomplished a revolution of the spirit which has not yet run its course. Yoḥanan recovered the whole of what was best in ancient teachings and reshaped it for the future. All that now was left was the workaday world. Politics had ended. The Temple lay in ruins. The piety lavished at its altar flowed wastefully to the ground. Jews ruled little more than their own home and hearth. The "house of Israel" now consisted of villages and towns, no longer of a state.

Yet Yoḥanan had long ago lived in just such a situation. By force of circumstance he had always addressed himself to precisely this setting. Though he had sought worldly influence, he had not had it outside his party. He spent his life a resentful sectarian, a spectator out of public life. So now when he spoke to the sorrowing people about the importance of private life and the centrality of their conduct with their fellow men, he spoke out of a mature, educated heart. He knew that life may be significantly lived outside the centers of power. He understood that in the end piety, devotion, and love for God flow from life to life, from heart to heart. The Temple provided merely one more opportunity to fulfill the word of the Creator.

"It is not the corpse which really renders unclean," he had said. Now he could have added, "It is not the Temple that calls forth man's piety. It is not the sacrifice of animals, but the contrite spirit, that God favors." Where had he learned such lessons? Both in his own experience and in Scripture which formed his perceptions of reality. He would have seen in his teachings no revolution, only a repetition of the teachings of Hosea whom he quoted, of the Psalmist, and above all, of Jeremiah.

The religion of Torah contained more than a message to the heart. It spoke of the transcendent worth of daily deeds, and therefore it required concern for humble and private life. It was not sufficient for Yoḥanan ben Zakkai to speak of loving-kindness to people who had no teachers, judges, or courts to tell them in concrete terms just what were the demands of loving-kindness. "Torah" contained laws as well as doctrines. It was through such laws that the Lawgiver had intended the doctrines to take worldly form. Good intention without good instruction could hardly provide guidance to the village folk. For this reason the Pharisees had always studied the law as well as the theology of Scripture. They concentrated their best energies upon the formation of the Torah's law as a moral force in the life of Israel. If, as Yoḥanan believed, when Israel would do the will of their Father in heaven, no nation or race would rule over them, then, the people had to know what God now required of them.

So teachers had to be taught and courts had to be established for the coming generations, or all the good words of the hour would be dissipated. To do this, Yoḥanan had to turn his attention to the very status of his own group in the Yavneh vineyard. Who were they? What was their authority? Did they speak merely as wise men? Or did they constitute a link in the great chain of tradition that had begun at Sinai?

VIII. Tall Pillar

i. Introduction

Above all, Yoḥanan now needed to show that he had a right to act. He and his colleagues had always claimed sole legitimacy. In their hands alone, they held, were the Scriptures and oral traditions inseparably revealed to Moses long ago. But how did he demonstrate that this was so? Those who formerly had heard the Pharisaic claim ignored it. The best way to win their attention was to make a decree and forcefully to effect it. What of the opposition? Priests survived the cataclysm. Remnants of the other groups and sects were still much in evidence. Yoḥanan looked for an occasion publicly and dramatically to assert his authoritative position and to force the opposition to accept it. The hour was not long in coming. It came on the New Year, probably the month following the Temple's destruction, as we shall see.

Yoḥanan ben Zakkai could hardly have undertaken to do what he was not absolutely sure to be the will of the Creator of heaven and earth. But given his certainty, he could hardly do otherwise than to carry out God's purpose. Long years of study on the Torah produced the necessary confidence. Yavneh on the New Year of 70 provided the first occasion for action.

ii. The Other Sects

The most pressing and yet soluble problems were liturgical. Holy days and festivals were formerly observed mainly in the Temple's sacrificial cult. Yoḥanan therefore decreed a series of specific modifications of law, necessitated by the disaster.

Somewhat later he and his successors came to define the authority of the academy which had earlier issued these ordinances. They then claimed that the academy held the authority formerly exerted by the Sanhedrin in Jerusalem. The Yavneh academy was now *the* high court capable of issuing authoritative enactments. And, they added, it really had always done just that. Yoḥanan's method was that of Hillel, Gamaliel I, and Simeon ben Gamaliel before him: to issue decrees on specific legal problems. His ordinances met some opposition, particularly from the priests, but in the main they came to be accepted.

The opposing parties had been weakened by the war. The Pharisees, in the persons of Yoḥanan and his disciples and succeeding colleagues at Yavneh, were eventually able to attain popular recognition. The other parties were doubtless represented among the people. From the destruction onward, however, the issues of Israel's religious life were debated in terms of the Pharisaic formulation of Judaism.

Christian Jews had escaped to Pella in Transjordan. The war marked the beginning of their separation from Jewry. The Herodians retired to their distant lands to rule mainly gentile populations. The Essene communes were devastated. Bereft of their separate communities, the surviving Essenes must have pursued their austere discipline with difficulty and transmitted it, if at all, with diminishing success.

The Sadducees suffered both from the present inadequacy of their doctrine and from their social position. They could cope only awkwardly with the problems posed by the destruction. The Sadducees could not provide answers to help the people meet the disaster, for they offered no promise of retribution or recompense in the world to come, as did the Pharisaic sages. Israel no longer worshiped at the Temple. The Sadducees, for whom the sacrificial system had been central, had no bastion prepared for retreat. Their view of law likewise must have rendered it almost impossible to legislate for the new era. They had denied the authority of oral tradition and held that interpretation was to be settled by *ad hoc* decisions of the court of the High Priest. The end of the high priestly authority therefore meant the end of their supreme court and of any means or authority able to legislate or to reinterpret the law. For the Sadducees, therefore, the authority to adapt the law to rapidly changing needs had disappeared. Furthermore, Sadducees, many of whom were upper-class priests and land-owners in the Judean region, lost considerable wealth in the war and concomitant social upheavals. Hence, while remnants of the Sadducees did survive the war, the policies and attitudes fostered by their party, even when relevant and congruent to the new dilemmas, received less attention than when, as earlier, they had been advanced by the leading men of Jerusalem.

iii. Advantages of the Pharisees

The Pharisees, on the contrary, had several particular ad-vantages. First of all, they advanced a comprehensive program for the religious life to replace the sacrificial system. Second, their doctrines of providence, life after death, retribution, and recompense for suffering offered meaningful consolation to men who daily lived with the ancient perplexity of mono-theism: Why do good men meet evil days? Third, their her-meneutical principles permitted them to give to ancient laws the broader construction which, under changing circumstances, was essential for the practical administration of the public polity. Fourth, they enjoyed the confidence of the Romans on account of the loyalism of some of their sages. They had the articulate support of Josephus to advocate their cause in Rome. Fifth, they also had the confidence of large parts of the nation. The ambivalence of their war policy, with Simeon tak-ing part in the revolutionary coalition and Yoḥanan among the pacifists, left them with the possibility of claiming extra-ordinary prescience, whatever the war's outcome. Sixth, the Pharisees now vigorously pressed their earlier claims to repre-sent the one legitimate authority in and interpretation of Judaism. In the absence of organized opposition from other groups the hour was particularly opportune to press such a claim, and, as it turned out, the Romans accepted it.

In time the Pharisees transformed their status. Earlier they had been a sectarian religious group among several competing parties. Now began the process by which they eventually came to constitute "normative Judaism." As the decades passed the larger part of the Jewish people came to embody what Pharisaism had conceived of as "holy congregation," that is, a community whose essential definition and foundation was the Mosaic faith as taught by Pharisaic sages. The Pharisees, finally, had the benefit of Yohanan ben Zakkai's leadership. They enjoyed the advantage of the central institution at Yavneh which began to take shape during his last years. Yohanan began the successful effort to bring the whole people to recognize the Pharisaic academy as legitimate successor and heir to the old Sanhedrin's authority. The reason was that, in his judgment, he and his colleagues and disciples had the obligation and right to reconstitute the social and religious order. Asserting this right, they carried on the prophetic teaching that Israel was to be more than an ethnic and cultural entity. Israel was to form a "kingdom of priests and a holy people," whose constitution was revelation and whose citizenship imposed ethical and religious obligations.

iv. Postwar Palestine

Yohanan was able to concentrate attention on liturgical and religious issues because most of the land and large parts of the people survived the war intact. This is indicated by the contrast between the *taqqanot* (ordinances) of Yohanan ben Zakkai at Yavneh, and those of the synod at Usha held after the collapse of the Bar Kokhba revolt. The war of 132–5 led to the destruction of the economic and social order. The synod took place about A.D. 140 after the Hadrianic persecutions, As at Yavneh, some ritual and calendrical questions were discussed, but the ordinances dealt chiefly with matters of family law, For example: parents must care for their children so long as they are minors; if a parent deeded his property to his sons during his lifetime, the sons must support their parents from the estate; the father must be patient in teaching his sons until they are twelve years of age—then he may send them out into the world. None of the ordinances of Yavneh reflect such appalling conditions. According to Josephus, up to one million five hundred thousand men, women, and children perished or were enslaved as a result of the rebellion. Although there is reason to consider this figure exaggerated, certainly large numbers were killed or enslaved. Several limited areas of the land had borne the brunt of the losses: in Jordan, Gamala; in Galilee, the northern strip of the Kinneret (Sea of Galilee), and the areas around Jotapata, including the town and around Sepphoris, but not including the city; Beth Shean and isolated areas in the Emeq; in Sharon, the region around Garvata; in the Plain, the region Antipatris and the sea, including Yaffo (Jaffa and southward to Lud (Lydda); in the Judean hills, the territories around Jericho, Jerusalem and Bet Netufah, north of Hebron, but not including Hebron. Even in these territories, however, many of the inhabitants fled before the fighting and survived the war.

The economy of the land suffered considerably. Famine, probably also a depression, followed the reconquest. Many families certainly lost their fortunes. The areas ravaged by the war, mainly agricultural lands, had to be restored to productivity. While trees and vineyards had been damaged, the fields had been refreshed by lying fallow. Large territories escaped damage. The economy sustained a greater war sixty-five years later, certainly an indication that it had substantially survived the earlier war with minimal effect. The Romans, moreover, applied and collected heavy taxes, a second indication that the economy retained substantial strength. Although there were great changes in the pattern of land tenure, as Jewish properties were expropriated, or confiscated for taxes, the former Jewish-held territories remained for the most part in Jewish hands, except in the immediate neighborhood of Jerusalem.

The country was not administered by a series of legates, including Sextus Vettulenus, commander of the Tenth Legion at Jerusalem, in 70–71; Lucilius Bassus, 71–72, who reduced the final pockets of resistance; Flacius Silva, 72–80; Salvidenus,

80–86; and Pompeius Longinus, 86. Except for the few details on military operations, however, nothing is known about the government of Judea. One fact is absolutely certain concerning Roman administration: they did not institute systematic religious persecutions. In wartime the Roman policy of tolerance may have been suspended. But afterward, only isolated incidents, such as an effort at Antioch to force Jews to desecrate the Sabbath, disturbed the free exercise of Judaism. The Romans did impose a *Fiscus Judaicus,* a head tax to be paid to Rome rather than, as earlier, to the Temple in Jerusalem. This tax represented symbolic submission to Rome, not the cessation of Israel's licit existence. The tax was abrogated before the turn of the century. Flavian religious policy did not, to be sure, encourage Jewish proselytism any more than it encouraged concerted persecution of Judaism. Jews retained their civil rights. Nothing altered the individual's right to enjoy whatever type of citizenship he had formerly held.

The social structure was considerably changed. Some men profited from the war to rise in social standing. A class of Jews arose who, through acquisition of large properties, was able to assume authority in villages and towns throughout the land. One reads about "lying judges," men who increased their capital at the expense of the depressed classes. The masses certainly bore the cost of the dislocation of the social economy. The standard of living declined.

Like Yohanan, Hananiah, prefect of the priests, testified to the general suffering after the war, saying:

And they shall be upon you for a sign and a wonder and upon your seed forever. Because you did not serve the Lord your God with joyfulness and with gladness of heart, by reason of the abundance of all things, therefore you shall serve thine enemy whom the Lord shall send against thee in hunger and in thirst and in nakedness and in want of all things (Deut. 28: 46) . *In hunger*—for example, when one craves food and cannot find even coarse bread, the heathen nations demand from him white bread and choice meat. *And in thirst*—for example, when one longs for drink and cannot find even a drop of vinegar or a drop of bitters, the heathen nations demand from him the finest wine in the world. *And in nakedness*—for example, when one is in need of clothing and cannot find even a wool shirt or a flaxen one, the heathen nations demand from him silks and the best cloth in the world. *And in want of all things*—that is, in want of light, of knife, of a table. Another interpretation: in want of vinegar and salt.

When at Yavneh, therefore, Yoḥanan ben Zakkai considered the situation in the land, he saw suffering and want, but he could well have observed that the nation had survived the calamity substantially intact. It could rely upon a damaged but viable economy. Palestine enjoyed strict, sometimes harsh, but bearable laws and a law-abiding government. Its social structure had sustained both loss in population and rearrangements of social status, but endured fundamentally unchanged by the revolutionary upheaval.

Yavneh itself was pleasantly situated. Consisting of two parts, a port and an inland borough, the town was a commercial center in the richest part of the plain. Nearby were Lud, Gimzo, Bene Braq, and Emmaus. The town held a large number of merchants and craftsmen, augmented by the loyalist refugees who settled after their escape and remained, having no better place to go after the war. The populace had been spared most of the trials of wartime. It had been a center of loyalism during the latter part of war. One may assume that the local populace did not bear ill feelings toward the refugee-rabbis and disciples. The warm climate of the coast permitted the sages to conduct most of their discussion in the open air. They could make the small living they needed either through crafts or in trade.

v. Yoḥanan's Enactments at Yavneh

At Yavneh Yoḥanan, his disciples, and colleagues had the first opportunity to effect their religious program. They hoped to transform the community of Israel in deed and in fact into the bearer and representation of the faith of Israel as they understood it. This social policy was the logical and natural consequence of their theology. Israel ought to be a holy people. In Jerusalem the Pharisees had been one among a great number of sects and had themselves exhibited internal divisions. Now, at Yavneh, they exerted what remained of Jewish autonomous authority with very little opposition from other Jewish groups. The Romans on the whole did not interfere with the operation of the court. The sages' agents or apostles acted in the manner of the collectors of the Temple taxes before the destruction.

How was authority handed on from the tribunal in Jerusalem to that at Yavneh? Yoḥanan, first, assumed the liturgical authority formerly vested *de facto* in the Temple priests to determine the proper calendar. Second, he exercised judicial and legal authority earlier held by the Sanhedrin in Jerusalem. Third, he performed certain rites formerly reserved for the Temple. Yoḥanan, of course, did not unveil at Yavneh a fully developed institution to replace the earlier court. He did not even legislate on a very wide range of subjects. His authority was not accepted everywhere without question. The local strong men simply ignored the sage's opinions. Yoḥanan enacted certain limited measures which at first may have applied only at Yavneh; this was the opinion of Eliezer ben Hyrcanus on the jurisdiction of one of the ordinances. In the time of Gamaliel II, the authority of the academy broadened. In succeeding decades it received widespread acceptance and *de jure* recognition from the Roman officials.

The broadening concerns of the later rabbis indicate a widening range of problems brought for their adjudication and a growing popular acceptance of their hegemony. Yoḥanan ben Zakkai himself left very few legal traditions. His students, Eliezer and Joshua, are among the most important legislators in Jewish history. What accounts for the difference? The answer may be found in the difference in authority exerted by his students and their generation. Before the destruction, when the Pharisees competed for power, the growth of their particular legal traditions may have been limited to the problems that came up before their own tribunal, with theoretical discussions of the rest of the law. While the Pharisees had their own traditions, the city's municipal courts had earlier dealt with the main matters of civil law which Jewish autonomy was competent to govern. Titus had noted that the Jews were permitted their own law, even after the procuratorial regime was established. Hence, while the Pharisees had and adhered to their own civil law and advanced their viewpoint on the common law, the country as a whole was not administered by them or in accordance with their opinions. After the destruction, as the sages successfully, though gradually, expanded the area of their authority, they met new and previously unconsidered issues of law. If, for example, they possessed general theoretical principles of law before the destruction, they had to apply them to a multiplicity of specific cases which they now were allowed to judge for the first time. The result was a perceptible expansion of the areas of their jurdical concern and, consequently, an increase in the disputes on individual cases. Yohanan's successors thus dealt with a wider variety of cases than he did. At Yavneh, Yohanan was concerned mainly with religious and ritual questions, while his students Eliezer and Joshua and his successor Gamaliel II had to adjudicate many other kinds of legal and theological matters. This accounts for the multiplicity of disputes between Eliezer and Joshua, both of whom studied with the same master. Yohanan might well have given them general principles on many questions, no opinions at all on some. Now they had to apply them. So one may understand both the conservatism of Eliezer and the broad legal constructions of Joshua. The extension of Pharisaic authority thus led to an expansion of Pharisaic law, formerly applied to a limited sect, and now to an entire nation.

The first dramatic issue came with the advent of the New Year shortly after A.D. 70, when the holy day happened to occur on the Sabbath. The outcome was the assertion that the academy at Yavneh possessed the same prerogative as the Temple in Jerusalem. The tradition states:

> If a festival day of the New Year fell on a Sabbath, they might blow the *shofar* in the Holy City, but not in the prov-

inces. After the Temple was destroyed, Rabban Yoḥanan ben Zakkai ordained that they might sound the *shofar* wherever there was a court.

Rabbi Eliezer said, "Rabban Yoḥanan ben Zakkai ordained it only for Yavneh."

They replied, "It is all one whether it was Yavneh or any other place in which there is a court."

Once it happened that Rosh Hashanah fell on the Sabbath, and all the villagers gathered in Yavneh to hear the *shofar*. Rabban Yoḥanan ben Zakkai said to the Men of Bathyra, "Let us sound the *shofar*."

They said to him, "Let us discuss [whether it is proper to do so or not]."

He said to them, "Let us sound the *shofar,* and afterward, let us discuss."

After they blew the *shofar,* they said to him, "Let us now discuss."

He said to them, "Already the *shofar* has been heard in Yavneh, and one does not debate after the fact."

While the *shofar* was blown in synagogue and Temple alike, if the New Year occurred on the Sabbath it might be sounded only in the Temple. Yoḥanan arrogated to the rabbinical courts the prerogative of the Temple. He thereby advanced a claim to broad authority for the sages' academies. The men of Bathyra were descendants of the Babylonian Jews whom Herod had settled in the northeast marches almost a century earlier. From them the chiefs of the Sanhedrin had been chosen before Hillel's time and that of Agrippa I and II likewise. During the war they were loyalists and settled at Yavneh, like Yoḥanan, to escape the war. They regarded themselves as authorities in just such matters as this. They were not prepared to accept either Yoḥanan's decision or the authority by which he made it. They demanded for themselves at least equivalent recognition. Hence the significance of this action in establishing the new institution is twofold. First, it represented a claim to recognition as a legitimate surrogate for the sanctuary. Second, it announced a policy of excluding from authority former Temple officials who came to claim it.

In a second series of enactments Yoḥanan met questions on the observance of Tabernacles, on the permission to eat new produce when the *omer* was no longer brought to Jerusalem, on receiving testimony concerning the new moon, on the manner of the priestly blessing, on the offering that a proselyte had formerly to bring to the Temple and on the disposal of the fourth-year fruits. All these matters required immediate attention on account of the destruction of the Temple on which their observance formerly depended. By his ordinances Yoḥanan preserved the memory of the cultic ritual without permitting its ancient forms to render obsolete the liturgical life of the people. The record of these ordinances follows:

> Before time, the *lulav* was carried seven days in the Temple, but in the provinces, on one day only. After the Temple was destroyed, Rabban Yoḥanan ben Zakkai ordained that in the provinces it should be carried seven days in memory of the Temple.
>
> Also he ordained that on the whole day of waving, it should be forbidden [to eat of the new produce]. [Scripture commands (Lev. 23:10), When you . . . reap the harvest, you shall bring the sheaf of the first fruits of your harvest to the priest, and he shall wave the sheaf before the Lord . . . . On the morrow after the Sabbath the priest shall wave it, and you shall eat neither bread, nor grain . . . until this same day, until you have brought the offering of your God. After the *omer* was offered, the new grain was immediately permitted to be eaten, but for those that lived away from Jerusalem, it was permitted only after mid-day.]
>
> After the Temple was destroyed, Rabban Yoḥanan ben Zakkai, ordained that it should be forbidden throughout the day of waving. [In the Temple days, it had been permitted earlier in the day because the people in the provinces knew that the offering would be brought in its proper time.]

On this action, the Talmud commented,

> What was the reason? Quickly may the Temple be rebuilt, and they may say, "Last year did we not eat when it was light in the east? Now too let us eat early in the morning." They

will not know that last year, there was no *omer,* and therefore, when it was light in the east, it was immediately permitted, but now that the *omer* is brought again in the Temple, the *omer,* and not the advent of the day, permits eating of new food.

Other liturgical enactments, touching the testimony for the new moon, were as follows:

Before time, they used to admit evidence about the new moon throughout the day of the new year. After sunset on the night after the 29th of Elul, they treated the coming day as a festival day, in case witnesses arrived the next day to report that the new moon was visible the preceding evening. If they did not come that day, the following day [also] was made a festival day, and the day before was considered as the 30th of Elul. Once the witnesses tarried so long in coming that the Levites were disordered in their singing [of the psalm at the daily whole offering. The usual afternoon daily whole offering was slaughtered at 2:30 P.M., but if it was the first of the month, additional offerings had to be brought (Num. 28:1) besides the daily whole offering. Therefore the offering was delayed as long as possible for the arrival of witnesses, to know whether or not additional offerings should be brought, and whether the Levites should sing the psalm for an ordinary day or for a festival day. This time, however, the delay was so long that there was not time for the prescribed psalm.]

So it was ordained that evidence could be admitted only until the afternoon offerings. And if witnesses came from the time of the afternoon offering and onward, then that day was kept holy and also the following day. After the Temple was destroyed, Rabban Yoḥanan ben Zakkai ordained that they might admit evidence about the new moon throughout the day [since it would not affect the singing of the proper psalms].

Rabbi Joshua ben Qorḥa said, "Rabban Yoḥanan ben Zakkai ordained this also, that wheresoever the chief of the court might be, witnesses should go only to the place of assembly [of the tribunal to testify about the new moon]."

Before time, they would profane the Sabbath to bring testimony on the new moon for all months. When the Temple was destroyed, Rabban Yoḥanan ben Zakkai said to them, "And do we now have a sacrifice [to offer in addition to that of the Sabbath] that we should permit the Sabbath day to be profaned?"

They ordained that they should not profane the Sabbath to bring testimony except for Nisan [on account of the coming Passover festival] and Tishre [account of the New Year] only.

Yoḥanan, on the other hand, preserved a Temple ritual in its precise form: "The priests are not permitted to go up [to bless the people with the priestly blessing] onto the platform with their shoes on [but rather, barefooted, as in the Temple]." What was the meaning of this ordinance? Yoḥanan required the priests to behave *as if* the synagogues at Yavneh and elsewhere *were* the Temple. In this decree he not only claimed for his court and its prayers the same prerogatives as had formerly applied in the Holy Sanctuary. He also forced the priests to conform to his will, if they hoped to continue their function of blessing the whole people. The priests had so recently lost the one responsibility that rendered them important. Now that they no longer sacrificed, or witnessed the sacrifices of others of their clan, what was left to them but the right to bless the people? They could not have wanted to listen to Yoḥanan. Even more, they could not have wanted to give up their sole remaining privilege. When it came to marriage, one recalls, they continued to ignore him. There was little he could do about it. But in the synagogue of Yavneh, and in those that followed its example, his will was supreme, and they had to obey.

To make matters worse, he also prohibited, for so long as the Temple should be destroyed, the consecration of money or objects for use of, or sacrifice in, the Temple:

> "A proselyte who converts in this time with the Temple in ruins must separate a quarter-coin for his bird offering [that is, he must put aside the cost of the offering even though he cannot actually make the sacrifice]."
>
> Rabbi Simeon ben Eleazar said, "Already Rabban Yoḥanan ben Zakkai has taken a poll against it and cancelled it, on account of [the possibility of] misusing [the money which had been set aside, for profane purposes]."

Rabbi Simeon said, "Rabban Yoḥanan ben Zakkai cancelled it [entirely], as it is taught, 'One does not declare holy, or to be evaluated [for the sanctuary] or declare *herem*, or raise up heave-offerings and tithes, and if a man declared holy, or evaluated, or *herem*, or gave heave-offering or tithes, the garments should be burned, the cattle should be set out to pasture [until they are blemished and no longer sacred].' "

Concerning all the ordinances of Yoḥanan ben Zakkai at Yavneh, Rabbi Judah said: "These things Rabban Yoḥanan ben Zakkai brought to pass in the world when the Temple was destroyed. When it will be rebuilt, these matters will return to their original condition."

vi. Yoḥanan's Policy at Yavneh

What do these ritual and liturgical ordinances tell us about the policy of Yoḥanan's academy at Yavneh? They fall into three groups: the first, on the celebration of the new moon and festivals and on receiving testimony concerning their proper dates; the second, on the priestly privileges; and the third, on the disposition of former emoluments of the Temple and city, the proselyte's offering and the fourth-year fruits. None of the categories reveals decisions on legal matters, but rather on strictly religious questions, which the Romans were probably content to leave to an autonomous Jewish court even during the first years after the destruction. All of them were clearly made necessary by the change in the liturgical situation after the destruction and did not represent innovations in law, so much as modifications in the face of the new and radically changed circumstances.

The first group reveals that Yoḥanan almost immediately began to try to fill the vacuum in the religious life which the Temple's destruction caused. Probably very soon after August, 70, possibly even in October of the same year, he decreed a memorial to the Temple: carrying the *lulav* all seven days, in memory of the Temple. Shortly thereafter, possibly in the spring of 71, he issued a second decree on the stricter observance of the law on the day of waving, again as a memorial to the Temple. He thereby announced immediately that the commandments which had depended on the Temple would continue to be observed even though the Temple was in ruins. Most significantly, he preserved the observance of the festival of Tabernacles and the commandment on consuming the new grain only after commencement of Passover, both of which had been dependent on the Temple rituals.

The other ordinances in the first group follow the same pattern. They indicate that Yoḥanan took account of the destruction by restoring older laws formerly abrogated on account of the Temple's needs. The testimony about the new moon of the New Year might be brought the entire day on which the testimony was to be expected, *but* the Sabbath might not be profaned in connection with bringing such testimony except for the New Year and the month in which Passover came (contrary to Rabban Gamaliel's ruling several decades earlier). The decree that the witnesses should come only to the court, despite the absence of its chief, may have represented an effort to strengthen its authority.

The ordinance on the priestly benediction, like that on sounding the *Shofar* on the New Year even though it coincided with the Sabbath, brought Yoḥanan into conflict with the priests. Indeed, it was likely to have been a very direct assertion of his authority over them. In the Temple the priests had been forbidden to go up onto the platform in their sandals to bless the congregation. By requiring the priests to continue this act of respect when they blessed the congregation outside the Temple, Yoḥanan declared his intention to issue rulings which would govern the priests as well as the laity. He tried to prevent the priests from utilizing their former prestige and the power of their blessing to acquire such a hold over the provincial congregations as they had had over Jerusalem. Furthermore, he emphasized that the congregation is holier than the priest, and therefore, even outside the sanctuary the priest must take his shoes off before going near to serve it, as Moses did before the bush.

The priestly blessing was made the service of a divine community, not a benefaction to be dispensed by the priest as he saw fit, and the act of service required the purifying act of washing. The priests were doubtless well aware of what Yoḥanan's policy meant.

Yoḥanan attempted to endow his new court with prerogatives hitherto reserved to the sanctuary—to preserve the memory and sanctity of the Temple, on the one hand, while providing for its temporary inaccessibility, on the other. He annulled a decree of Gamaliel I. He apparently took into his own jurisdiction the problems connected with the disposition of sacred offerings which could no longer reach the altar.

The traditions preserved nine enactments in all, covering the following matters: (1) the *Shofar*; (2) the *lulav*; (3) the Day of Waving; (4) receiving testimony on the eve of the New Year; (5) receiving testimony even when the head of the court is absent; (6) not profaning the Sabbath to give such testimony, except for the New Year and Passover; (7) the priestly blessing; (8) the proselyte's offering; (9) the fourth-year fruits. I wonder whether these were the only such enactments, for the multiplicity of problems, even in the limited area of religious and liturgical affairs, must have necessitated many others. To suppose that his teachings and the actions of his court were limited to the handful reported by rabbinic tradition is hardly reasonable. What is preserved of his legal record clearly represents what the members of the court of Gamaliel II saw fit to recall. Yoḥanan must have envisaged a legal reconstruction of Judaism along lines which were subsequently modified.

Yoḥanan may have proposed to declare in abeyance all those parts of the law which depended solely on the Temple for their performance or importance (along with ordinances numbered 1, 2, 3, 4, 5, 6, 7, 8 and 9 above); modified those laws which might still be useful in the synagogue liturgy (numbers 1, 2, 3 above); and rejected priestly privileges (number 7 above). Such a policy would have been utterly unacceptable to the priests. Disappearance of other references to Yoḥanan's enactments as legally valid precedent may have been the price which Gamaliel II later had to pay to secure priestly cooperation.

We cannot ignore the fact that whatever we know about Yoḥanan ben Zakkai has been handed on to us by later generations. They recalled what they *could* believe about him, and they could believe only what made sense in their own situation. People did not keep alive traditions, sayings, or stories because they were antiquarians, but because they thought them holy or important. A story was a precedent and a precedent was binding. No one was willing to "remember" what he could not to begin with believe to be true. So the few ordinances we have are those that Gamaliel II and his court transmitted or were unable to suppress.

What did Yoḥanan achieve? Through legislation on trivialities he acquired for his new court rights and privileges formerly reserved for the Temple in Jerusalem. That did not mean he did not mourn for the Temple or hope for its restoration. Quite to the contrary, he did everything he could to preserve the memory and sanctity of the Temple, but he made arrangements for the period in which the Temple would no longer be accessible. He took into his own jurisdiction problems connected with the disposition of sacred offerings which could no longer reach the altar.

He chose a middle way. He prayed for the rebuilding of the Temple, but he took full account of the needs of the generation which had to live without it. He did not expect that centuries would pass without the restoration of a permanent Temple in Jerusalem. He showed how to carry on for one year, or ten years, or forever.

vii. Opposition

Most of the sages who survived the destruction succeeded in doing so *precisely* because they were *not* in Jerusalem when it fell. According to Josephus' account, very few adult males who were in Jerusalem when the Romans conquered it survived death and escaped slavery (and so could even appear in a Pharisaic court within the next decade). Apart from the internecine strife, in which, certainly, some of the Pharisaic moderates must have fallen, Josephus records a vastly increased mortality rate, famine, epidemics, execution of the Temple priests, thorough search of all hiding places, and indiscriminate slaughter: "Pouring into the alleys, sword in hand, they massacred indiscriminately all whom they met, and burnt the houses with all who had taken refuge within . . . while they pitied those who had perished [of famine], they had no similar feelings for the living, but running everyone through who fell in their way, they choked the alleys with corpses, and deluged the whole city with blood." Almost everybody in the court of Gamaliel II probably had either fled Jerusalem during the early stages of the war or had been absent from the first and stayed away. The dominant, prowar party of the Pharisees in Jerusalem was almost annihilated, and this is one of the reasons that there is so little reference at the court of Yoḥanan or of Gamaliel II to the opinions of sages of the period before 70.

One sage, however, very likely did remain in Jerusalem until the end and only reached Yavneh with great difficulty. That was Gamaliel II, son of Simeon ben Gamaliel and heir to the prestige and authority of the house of Hillel, and through it, of David. His relationship with Yoḥanan is extremely unclear. While Yoḥanan may have acted to found and lead the academy because Gamaliel was unable to assume authority, some, including possibly Gamaliel himself, may have regarded Yoḥanan's decrees as acts of usurpation. In any case, while Yoḥanan was still alive, Gamaliel replaced him. Gamaliel probably could not have come to Yavneh before the close of hostilities in 73, and he returned during the term of L. Flavius Silva, 72–80, or, at the very latest, that of M. Salvidenus, 80–86. How he regarded the achievement of Yoḥanan there, one simply does not know. His later relationships with Joshua and Eliezer, which were not cordial, would suggest that Gamaliel had to cope with enmity from Yoḥanan's old and loyal disciples, very possibly on Yoḥanan's account.

Whatever the opposition he faced, Yoḥanan clearly considered himself the possessor of the legitimate internal autonomy available to Israel. He instituted the formal appointment of his disciples as *rabbis,* giving to the sages for the first time an official status within the Jewish polity: "At first each one would appoint (ordain) his own students, as Rabban Yoḥanan ben Zakkai ordained Rabbi Eliezer and Rabbi Joshua, and Rabbi Joshua appointed Rabbi 'Aqiba, and Rabbi 'Aqiba, Rabbis Meir and Simeon. In this action he created a new form of legitimization for Jewish leadership within the Pharisaic tradition. Before then the sages were recognized through neither title nor official status. Afterward, they constituted an authoritative and continuing class of officials in Jewish life.

viii. Defender of the Faith

Yoḥanan also represented the Jewish faith to gentiles with whom he came into contact. He debated questions of Jewish doctrine and scriptural interpretation. While we cannot determine exactly with whom he debated, some of these discussions possibly took place when he was in Yavneh where there were larger numbers of gentiles, rather than at Jerusalem where such contacts would have been limited. Certainly at Yavneh he must have come into contact with Roman authorities.

The effort has been made to identify his antagonist with a Roman official, Antonius Julianus, procurator of Judah during the siege of Jerusalem, and alleged author of a book, *De Judaeis,* in which the sufferings of the Jews were presented as punishment for their having abandoned God and his discipline. Unfortunately, all that is known of this book is one sentence in the writings of Minucius Felix. On so small a basis, one cannot accept such an identification.

The record of the conversations contains no element of reproach against the Jews for their rebellion, but rather it presents mainly the kinds of exegetical debates common in this period. One reported conversation is as follows:

> It happened that a certain gentile asked Rabban ben Zakkai, "We have festival seasons and you have festival seasons. We

have Calendae, and Saturnalia, and Kratesis, and you have Passover, Pentecost, and Tabernacles. What is the day on which we and you rejoice together?"

Rabban Yoḥanan said to him, "That is the day on which rain falls. How do we know? It is written (Ps. 65:13), *The meadows clothe themselves with grain, they shout and sing together for joy.* And what is written after this? *Make a joyful noise to God, all the earth, sing the glory of his name* (Ps. 66:1)."

So Yoḥanan told his questioner that it was the natural order of the world which Jews and gentiles celebrate together. All men alike rejoice when it rains. To appreciate what Yoḥanan actually was saying, we must recall Jeremiah's stress upon the meaning of the natural order of the world. As long as the rains fall and the tides keep their boundaries at the shore of the sea, that long will the covenant between Israel and their Father in heaven remain valid. When the covenant fails, so too will the regular order of nature be corrupted. Simple and neutral acts which all men do together testify in the end, therefore, to the abiding validity of the covenant between God and Israel through the Torah. Yoḥanan's reply thus reaffirmed that despite the destruction of the Temple, the covenant remained valid, and he further implied that when gentiles rejoice along with Jews on a rainy day, they unknowingly delighted in a sign of the Jews' special relationship to God. It was an ironic reply to the gentile's question.

With the destruction of the Temple, Jews must have found it necessary to explain their convictions to a wider audience. The catastrophe was, after all, public knowledge widely commented on. Rome had invested great wealth in the project, and throughout the world the imperial war and its aftereffects were everywhere discussed. If before that time the Jews were seen to possess strange, but on the whole either reasonable or merely bizarre beliefs and practices, afterward they stood apart and alone. Gentiles no longer questioned the uniqueness, or separatism, of the Jews, no longer wondered about this peculiar rite or that. Now they reflected upon the more general and striking fact that the Jews had opposed the ruler of civilization. Contact between Roman administrators and troops and Palestinian Jewry was considerably increased, moreover, with the intervening layer of Jewish bureaucrats—Temple authorities, Herodians—removed. Yoḥanan's participation in disputations signifies the beginning of a new era in the Jews' relationships to other peoples. Before this time they lived pretty much as did other groups. The chief facts of their life corresponded to those of other nations: land, cult, priesthood, holy book, common culture. Now they persisted, and would continue to persist, as an anomaly among the societies of men. And as such, they would draw to themselves the attention of curiosity-seekers, philosophers, scholars, and troublemakers. Pharisaic masters, and Yoḥanan to begin with, now undertook the additional task of representing, and defending, not only "Torah" as they taught it, but the Jews as a group.

ix. Conclusion

This much is known about Yoḥanan ben Zakkai at Yavneh. He began to build a new center of autonomous government. He decided certain ritual and religious questions. He taught his disciples. He debated on occasion with gentiles in the town. If Yoḥanan had never gone to Yavneh, he would probably be almost forgotten in Jewish history. The detailed record of his activity there, however, has barely managed to reach posterity. The course of his last few years of life is not much clearer. He retired to Beror Ḥeil, a village in the foothills of Judea, and remained until his death. There he handed down decisions in cases that came before him. By renouncing power in Yavneh, he saved what he had founded, for he dissolved opposition to the academy based on enmity toward himself and his ambiguous record. Yoḥanan cleared the way for Gamaliel II to assume the leadership of the broader part of the nation.

So ended the brief period of Yoḥanan's worldly power. A man of contention, he withdrew when he saw others better able to carry forward what he had begun. His life was drawing

to a close. What had he to show for the effective years?—
a court for whose sake he again had to go into exile, a few
students, a few laws about the rites and worship of Israel.
He had changed some trivial details of the law, established a
few principles, and in the face of opposition, retired to live
out his final months, perhaps a year or two, again in isolation
from the great center of activity.

One morning, accompanied by his faithful students Joshua
and Eliezer, he turned his face toward the sun. Together they
walked into the hills. Resigned that his task, whether done or
not, had best be continued by others, he exiled himself from
Yavneh. His son had died long ago, and so, I imagine, had his
wife. Lonely, tired, carried by the will of others, much as
Jeremiah had been brought to the border of Egypt, he went
off to build another court and to die.

What had Yavneh meant to him? We see it as the lasting
link between one age and the next. We see him as the man
who forged that link. But could he have seen it so? Perhaps
Yavneh was his sapling, and now, he thought, was the time to
go forth.

He had left Hillel's academy for Galilee. Others stayed on
in the center of Jerusalem. He lived, lonely and ignored, and
left a bitter curse. To be sure, he did not curse Yavneh, nor
would he have wanted to. But were matters otherwise so very
different? In Galilee, he had been ignored. In Yavneh, he
faced deep hostility. Which was preferable? In Galilee, his
student possessed skills more important to people than his
own. In Yavneh only his disciples could complete what he
started.

His mind must have turned to still another leave-taking—
this one more vivid in his memory—the day he had been
carried out of Jerusalem in a coffin, like his son in earlier
years. In the eyes of many, he was a traitor who went to enter
into negotiations with the enemy. Then, at least, he had sought
to save what could be saved. Now his life was behind him.
Then, he might have conceived a great mission ahead. Now
what remained for him to do? Only one cryptic account tells

what he actually did in Beror Ḥeil: "If you are looking for a good court of justice, then go to Yoḥanan ben Zakkai in Beror Ḥeil." At the brink of death, he steadfastly founded yet another schoolhouse, that and his disciples his only legacy to the world.

EPILOGUE
Father of the Future

Yoḥanan ben Zakkai died probably a decade or so after the destruction of Jerusalem, not a martyr, but more appropriately, in bed, surrounded by his loyal disciples. Having chosen to concern himself with day-to-day affairs, he offered the promise contained in the moral conduct of commonplace life as Israel's true consolation. A martyr's death would have been incongruent to such a teaching. His death was reported as follows:

> In his last hours, Rabban Yoḥanan ben Zakkai kept weeping out loud.
> "O master," his disciples exclaimed, "O tall pillar, light of the world, mighty hammer, why art thou weeping?"
> He said to them, "Do I then go to appear before a king of flesh and blood, whose anger, if he should be angry with me, is but of this world? and whose chastising, if he should chastise me, is but of this world? Whom I can, moreover, appease with words or bribe with money? Verily, I go rather to appear before the King of Kings of Kings, the Holy One, blessed be he, whose anger, if he should be angry with me, is of this world, and the world to come, and whom I cannot appease with words or bribe with money! Moreover I have before me two roads, one to Paradise and one to Gehenna, and I know not whether he will sentence me to Gehenna or admit me into Paradise. And of this a verse says, *Before him shall be sentenced all those that go down to the dust, even he that cannot keep his soul alive"* (Ps. 22:30) —and should I not weep?"
> They said to him, "Master, bless us!"
> He said to them, "May it be God's will that the fear of Heaven be upon you as much as the fear of flesh and blood."
> They said to him, "Just so much?"

He answered, "Would that it were so. Know ye that when a man sins a sin, he says, 'I hope no *man* sees me.' "

And as he breathed his last, he said, "Clear the house of vessels which can receive corpse-uncleanness, and prepare a throne for Hezekiah, king of Judah, who cometh."

Yoḥanan thus blessed his students with a blessing based on his earlier teaching to them, that the robber who steals in broad daylight is a better man than the thief who steals by night, for the one regards God and man as equals, and the other fears not God, but only man. He ended his life with a characteristic reminder of the humble necessities imposed by the laws of ritual purity on those who kept them. In a moment, the house would be unclean by reason of corpse-uncleanness; therefore, clear out objects which will receive it. He expressed the disquiet he felt with the prospect close at hand of going to appear before God.

We know little about Yoḥanan's spiritual biography, but it seems clear that on the long road from Jerusalem, through 'Arav and Yavneh to Beror Ḥeil, he had passed through a valley of deep shadows and dark uncertainties. Finally he told his students with his dying breath to prepare a throne for Hezekiah king of Judah, who, it was held, would herald a better day. Yoḥanan had earlier opposed despairing trust in God's immediate intervention into human affairs, and yet he died with the messianic hope on his lips. Yoḥanan here gave expression to his view of his own achievement. He did not regard his program of Torah, commandments, and acts of loving-kindness, or his institution at Yavneh, as the final stages in man's salvation, but only as interim measures. He looked forward, as did other Jews, to the Messiah's coming. Accordingly, he had offered this paradigm for Judaism: "If you have a sapling in your hand, and one comes to say that the Messiah is here, plant the sapling, and then go forth to receive him." At Yavneh, Yoḥanan had planted his sapling. In the moment of death, he looked to receive him who must come.

NOTES ON
SOURCES AND TRANSLATIONS

Translations from Hebrew are my own, except as indicated.

201